Sean McManus

Scratch Programming

in easy steps

covers Scratch 2.0 and Scratch 1.4

In easy steps is an imprint of In Easy Steps Limited
16 Hamilton Terrace · Holly Walk · Leamington Spa
Warwickshire · United Kingdom · CV32 4LY
www.ineasysteps.com

In Easy Steps Limited supports The Forest Stewardship Council (FSC),
the leading international forest certification organisation. All our titles
that are printed on Greenpeace approved FSC certified paper carry the
FSC logo.

MIX
Paper from
responsible sources
FSC
www.fsc.org   FSC® C020837

Printed and bound in the United Kingdom

ISBN 978-1-84078-612-5

Contents

Foreword by Mitchel Resnick

Mitchel Resnick is Professor of Learning Research at the MIT Media Lab.

Is it important for all children to learn how to write? After all, very few children grow up to become journalists, novelists, or professional writers. So why should everyone learn to write?

Of course, such questions seem silly. People use writing in all parts of their lives: to send birthday messages to friends, to jot down shopping lists, to record personal feelings in diaries. The act of writing also engages people in new ways of thinking. As people write, they learn to organize, refine, and reflect on their ideas. It's clear that there are powerful reasons for everyone to learn to write.

I see coding (computer programming) as an extension of writing. The ability to code allows you to "write" new types of things – interactive stories, games, animations, and simulations. And, as with traditional writing, there are powerful reasons for everyone to learn to code.

The recent surge of interest in learning to code, reflected in sites like codecademy.com and code.org, has focused especially on job and career opportunities. It is easy to understand why: the number of jobs for programmers and computer scientists is growing rapidly, with demand far outpacing supply.

But I see much deeper and broader reasons for learning to code. In the process of learning to code, people learn many other things. They are not just learning to code, they are coding to learn. In addition to learning mathematical and computational ideas (such as variables and conditionals), they are also learning strategies for solving problems, designing projects, and communicating ideas. These skills are useful not just for computer scientists but for everyone, regardless of age, background, interests, or occupation.

Six years ago, my research group at the MIT Media Lab launched the Scratch programming language and online community in an effort to make coding accessible and appealing to everyone.

...cont'd

We've been amazed with the diversity and creativity of the projects. Take a look at the Scratch website and you'll find animated stories, virtual tours, science simulations, public-service announcements, multimedia art projects, dress-up games, paint editors, and even interactive tutorials and newsletters.

We find that active members of the Scratch community start to think of themselves differently. They begin to see themselves as creators and designers, as people who can make things with digital media, not just browse, chat, and play games. While many people can read digital media, Scratchers can write digital media.

Scratch community members also begin to see the world in new ways. As one 11-year-old Scratcher wrote on a public blog: "I love Scratch. Wait, let me rephrase that – Scratch is my life. I have made many projects. Now I have what I call a 'Programmer's mind.' That is where I think about how anything is programmed. This has gone from toasters, car electrical systems, and soooo much more."

It has been exciting to watch what young people are creating and learning with Scratch. But this is just the beginning. The new version of the Scratch programming language and online community moves Scratch into the cloud, enabling people to program, save, share, and remix Scratch projects directly in a web browser. The new version also adds many new features to enhance opportunities for creativity and collaboration.

But we are aware that new features and capabilities are not enough. The biggest challenges for the future are not technological but cultural and educational. Ultimately, what is needed is a shift in mindsets, so that people begin to see coding not only as a pathway to good jobs, but as a new form of expression and a new context for learning.

Mitchel Resnick

This is an edited version of an article that was originally published at Edsurge (www.edsurge.com).

Hot tip

The book has been written so that each chapter teaches you something new, and builds on the previous chapters. For that reason, the best way to use this book is to work through the chapters in the right order.

1 Introducing Scratch

In this chapter, you'll get started with Scratch, including learning about the different versions, meeting some of the blocks used to give instructions, and creating your first program. You also learn how to save your work, and load example projects by others.

What is Scratch?

Programming is the art of writing instructions to tell a computer what to do. A set of instructions is called a program. The instructions are written in what's known as a programming language, and there are thousands to choose from.

Scratch is a programming language that is perfect for making games, animations, interactive stories and other visually rich programs. It provides a great introduction to programming for people of all ages. It's widely used in schools and colleges, but Harvard University has also used it in higher education at its Summer School. I've led workshops for adults where Scratch provided a friendly introduction to the kind of creative problem solving that programmers do all the time.

Scratch is easier to use than most other programming languages for a number of reasons:

Hot tip

Scratch doesn't cost anything and it works on Windows, Mac and Linux computers.

- You don't have to remember or type any commands: they're all on screen, so you can just drag and drop them.

- Commands fit together like jigsaw pieces, so there are strong visual hints about how you can combine them.

- Error messages are rare. Because Scratch commands lock together, programs always make some kind of sense. It is possible to still write programs with logical errors in, if they don't do what you expected, but Scratch guides you to write things that work, rather than nagging you when they don't.

- The commands are color-coded and categorized, so you can easily find a command when you need it.

- The commands in Scratch simplify common activities in games, such as testing whether a missile has hit an alien (collision detection), or rotating a character on screen.

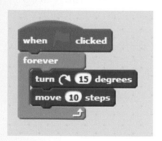

Above: A simple Scratch program, showing how the color-coded commands lock together.

In short, Scratch is designed for your success. It enables you to quickly see results from your work, and even includes graphics and sounds you can use so you can get started right now. Many other programming languages require you to learn text commands, and strict rules about how you can use them. Scratch doesn't. That means you can focus your energy instead on the fun stuff: dreaming up ideas for new programs, working out how to build them, designing them, and sharing them with friends.

Which version of Scratch?

There are two versions of Scratch that are in popular use. In this book, I'll tell you about both.

Scratch 2.0

Scratch 2.0 is the latest version of Scratch, which was introduced in May 2013. I recommend you use Scratch 2.0 if you can. This version makes it easier for people to share their projects, take a look at each other's projects, and adapt them (or "remix" them).

You don't need to install any software to use Scratch 2.0: it runs inside your browser, using an Internet connection. Scratch 2.0 needs a computer that can run the Adobe Flash Player, though, so it doesn't work on some mobile devices (including the iPhone and iPad) and some lower-powered devices (including the Raspberry Pi). Most other computers run Scratch 2.0 fine.

There is also a version of Scratch 2.0 that you can download from the Scratch website and install on your computer, so you can use it without an Internet connection. There are no official plans to bring Scratch 2.0 to the Raspberry Pi, though.

Scratch 1.4

Scratch 1.4 is the previous version of Scratch, and it is software you install on your computer. You can download it for Windows, Mac and Linux at **http://scratch.mit.edu/scratch_1.4/** This version of Scratch found a whole new audience with the meteoric rise of the Raspberry Pi, the stripped-down Linux-based computer for hobbyists and education (see photo).

Beware

If you're using the Scratch 2.0 website, I recommend using the Google Chrome browser with it. I experienced some bugs using Internet Explorer, which disappeared when I started using Chrome. You can download Chrome for free at **www.google.com/chrome**

Hot tip

ScratchJR is a simplified tablet version of Scratch for children aged 5.7. See **www.scratchjr.org**

Hot tip

If you have a weak Internet connection, or none at all, you might prefer to use the downloadable version of Scratch to the browser-based version.

Starting on the Raspberry Pi

Scratch is included with the recommended version of the Linux operating system, called Raspbian. I'll assume you've got your Raspberry Pi connected up and working already:

1 Switch on your Raspberry Pi and log in. The default login is **pi**, and the default password is **raspberry**

2 When you see the prompt pi@raspberrypi ~ $, enter **startx** and press the Enter or Return key

3 The LXDE desktop appears (see picture). The large Raspberry is just a background image, so you might see something different. You might also see different icons

4 Double-click the Scratch icon, which has a picture of a cat on it. In the screenshot below, it's in the top-left corner of the screen

5 You can also start Scratch using the Programs Menu, as also shown below: click the button in the bottom-left to open the menu, click the Programming folder, and finally, click Scratch

Hot tip

If you don't have Scratch installed on your Raspberry Pi, you can install it. After logging in, enter the command:

sudo apt-get update && sudo apt-get install scratch

That command will also update Scratch to the latest version, if Scratch is already installed.

Beware

The commands on the Raspberry Pi are case-sensitive, so it won't work if you type in Startx (with a capital S), for example.

12

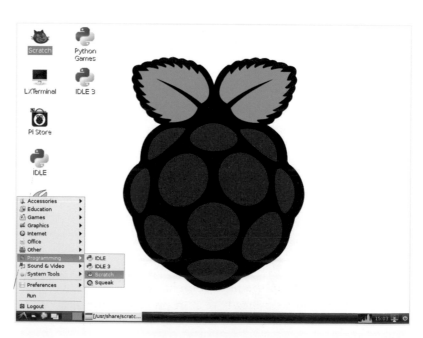

Creating a Scratch account

Before you begin to program with Scratch 2.0, I recommend you create an account for the Scratch website. Here's how:

1 Open a web browser, such as Google Chrome

2 Enter the website address **http://scratch.mit.edu/** in your address bar, usually at the top of the screen

3 Click **Join Scratch** in the top-right

4 Make up a username. Scratch is used by young people (among others), so the site advises members to protect their privacy by not using real names. You can't change your username later, so choose wisely

5 Pick a password and enter it twice. The second time is to make sure you've typed it correctly. Use a mixture of upper and lower case, numbers and symbols to make it more secure. Click the **Next** button

6 Enter your date of birth, gender, country and email address. This personal information is used to help you recover your password if you forget it, and is used by the Scratch team to understand who uses Scratch. It doesn't appear on the website anywhere. Click the **Next** button

7 Click **OK Let's Go!** and you will be logged in. Simply click **Create** on the navigation bar at the top of the screen, and you're ready to start programming!

Hot tip

The design of websites can change from time to time, so don't worry if you see variations in the sign-up process when you do it.

Hot tip

You can try Scratch 2.0 by just going to the website and clicking Create at the top of the screen. If you use an account, though, the website will automatically save your work for you.

Hot tip

When you return to the site next time, you can just click "Sign in" in the top right to get to all your projects.

Using the Scratch screen

To start using Scratch 2.0, visit **http://scratch.mit.edu/** in your web browser and click **Create** at the top of the screen. To start using Scratch 1.4, double-click its icon on your desktop.

The most obvious difference between the two versions of Scratch is the way the screen is laid out. With the exception of the Backpack (a new feature in Scratch 2.0), all the same elements are there, but they've been juggled around a bit. The background colors have been lightened in Scratch 2.0 too. This page shows the screen layout in Scratch 2.0, and the facing page shows the screen layout in Scratch 1.4.

The main parts of the screen are:

● **Stage:** This is where you can see your animations and games in action. When Scratch starts, there's a large orange cat in the middle of the Stage. In Scratch 2.0, the Stage is on the left, whereas in Scratch 1.4, the Stage is on the right.

● **Sprite List:** The cat is a 'sprite', which is like a character or object in a game. Your project might include lots of sprites, such as the player's spaceship, invading aliens and a missile. In the Sprite List, you can see all the sprites that are in your project, and click them to switch between them. In both versions of Scratch, the Sprite List is underneath the Stage.

Tabs

Scripts Area

Stage

Blocks Palette

Sprite List

Backpack

Right: Scratch 2.0

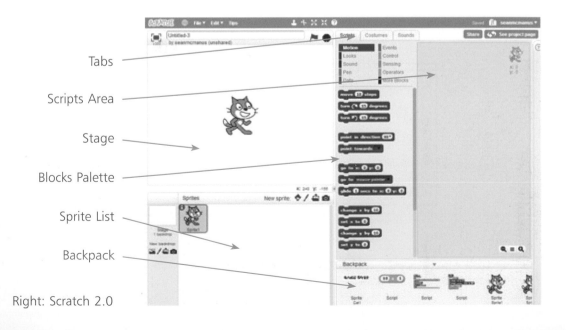

- **Blocks Palette:** In Scratch, you give the computer commands by using blocks, which are instructions that fit together like jigsaw pieces. The Blocks Palette presents you with all the blocks you can use. When you start Scratch, you can see the Motion blocks, which are color-coded in dark blue, and are used for moving sprites around the Stage. You can browse a different set of blocks in the Blocks Palette by clicking one of the buttons above it, such as the **Looks** button or the **Sound** button.

- **Scripts Area:** The Scripts Area is where you make your programs in Scratch, by assembling blocks there. This area expands to fill the screen space available, so if you use a larger monitor, the Scripts Area will be bigger.

- **Backpack:** The Backpack is a new feature in Scratch 2.0, which you can find underneath the Blocks Palette and Scripts Area. Click it to open it. It works a bit like a clipboard. You can copy scripts or sprites to it by dragging them there and dropping them. If you want to use them, just drag them from the Backpack back into your project. Your Backpack works across all your projects, so it's a great way to copy sprites or bits of program between different projects.

Don't forget

You'll see all these elements in action soon, so don't worry about memorizing the screen layout. This section is just to help you get your bearings. Remember that these pages are here to refer to at any time.

15

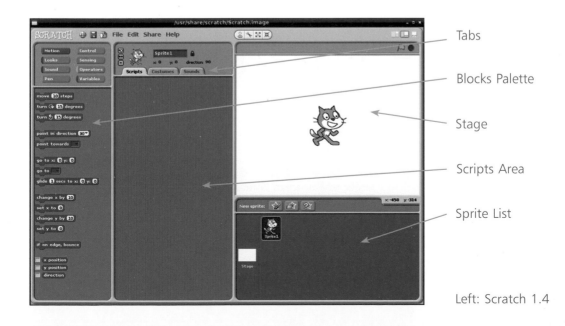

Tabs

Blocks Palette

Stage

Scripts Area

Sprite List

Left: Scratch 1.4

Exploring the blocks

Before we start making a program, try experimenting with a few blocks to see what they do:

1 Click the **Motion** button above the Blocks Palette to show the Motion blocks. This button is selected when you first start Scratch

2 In the Blocks Palette, click the **move 10 steps** block. The cat on the Stage moves in the direction it's facing, to the right. Each time you click the block, the cat moves once. This block only changes the cat's position, though: you won't see its legs move

16

3 The number of steps is how far across the screen you want the cat to move. Click the number 10 and change it to something else. Try 50 and when you click the block, the cat moves five times as far. Whenever you see a white hole in a block, you can change what's in it

4 Rotate the cat by clicking the **turn clockwise 15 degrees** block. To change the angle of the turn, change the number. Remember to click the block to actually make the cat turn. When you click the **move 10 steps** block next time, the cat walks in its new direction

Above: The cat on the Stage, after I clicked Turn Clockwise 15 Degrees.

5 If the cat gets to the edge of the Stage, drag it back again with your mouse pointer. Click the cat, hold the mouse button down, move the cat, and then release the mouse button to drop it in place

6 Click the **Pen** button above the Blocks Palette

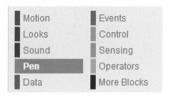 

Hot tip

All these blocks are explained later in the book, but for now it's worth spending a few minutes exploring some of the commands you can give the cat.

7 Click the **pen down** block. Now, if you click the Motion button and click the blocks to move the cat around, it will leave a line behind it wherever it goes. There is also a **pen up** block you can use to turn this effect off again

8 If you're using Scratch 2.0, click the **Looks** button above the Blocks Palette

9 In Scratch 2.0, click the **next costume** block to see the cat's legs move, so it appears to run on the spot. Costumes are just different pictures a sprite can have, and the cat has two that show its legs in different positions (see below)

Hot tip

In Scratch 1.4, the cat only has one costume, but I'll show you how to add additional costumes in Chapter 5.

17

Changing the backdrop

Before we make our first program, let's change the background of the Stage to something more inspiring. The way you do this is different in Scratch 2.0 and Scratch 1.4.

Choosing a backdrop in Scratch 2.0

1 To the left of the Sprites List, there is a panel for the Stage. Underneath the heading New Backdrop, click the first icon to choose a backdrop from the library. The other icons enable you to paint a backdrop, upload a picture from your computer, or use your webcam to take a photo

2 When the library opens, click the themes and categories on the left to view different backdrops available, and use the scrollbar on the right to see more designs. Click the Nature theme

3 Click the hill image, and then click the **OK** button

4 Your backdrop is added to the Stage, behind the cat, and the Paint Editor opens on the right so you can edit the background if you want to. We'll look at the Paint Editor in Chapter 4

18

Choosing a background in Scratch 1.4

1 To the left of the Sprite List is a white icon that represents your blank Stage. Click it to start

2 Click the **Backgrounds** tab above the Scripts Area, then click the **Import** button

3 Use the file browser to explore the backgrounds available. Double-click a folder icon to look inside that folder. To go back to the previous folder, click the **up arrow** indicated below

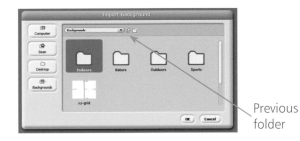

Previous folder

4 Go into the Nature folder and use the scrollbar on the right to find the hill picture. Click it and then click **OK**

5 Your background is added to the Stage, behind the cat

Creating your first program

Hot tip

If you click and drag a block that's joined to other blocks in the Script Area, it will break away from them, and carry all the blocks underneath it with it.

Beware

You can move blocks around the Scripts Area, but if you drag them into the Blocks Palette, they'll be deleted.

Don't forget

Make sure the blocks snap together, otherwise they won't work as one script. If they don't snap together, they're not close enough.

When you click blocks in the Blocks Palette, the cat moves immediately, so this is good for testing what blocks do, but not useful for making a program. A program is a set of repeatable instructions that you can store up to carry out later. For our first Scratch program, let's make the cat walk down the hill:

1 We're going to write a program for the cat so click the cat in the Sprite List

2 Next, check that the Scripts Area is open. If the Scripts Area is empty, you're ready. If it shows costumes or sounds instead, click the **Scripts** tab. In Scratch 2.0, the **Scripts** tab is above the Blocks Palette. In Scratch 1.4, it's above the Scripts Area

3 Click the **Motion** button above the Blocks Palette

4 You make a program by dragging blocks into the Scripts Area from the Blocks Palette. To do this for your first block, click the **turn clockwise 15 degrees** block in the Blocks Palette, hold the mouse button down, move the mouse pointer into the Scripts Area and then release the mouse button. This first block will point our cat downhill, ready for its walk

5 Click the **move 10 steps** block in the Blocks Palette, drag it into the Scripts Area and drop it underneath the **turn clockwise 15 degrees** block. They will snap together. When blocks are joined like this they make what's known as a "script". A sprite can have more than one script, and a program might include lots of sprites with several scripts

6 Click the **Control** button above the Blocks Palette. Control blocks are used to decide when things should happen. Drag the **wait 1 secs** block into the Scripts Area and snap it underneath the other two blocks. This block adds a 1 second delay. Without it, our cat will move so fast, it'll appear to just jump from the start of his walk to the end. Slowing him down enables us to see what's going on. You can make him walk a bit faster by changing the delay from 1 second to 0.5 seconds

7 Right-click the **move 10 steps** block, and when the menu opens, choose **Duplicate**. This copies the block plus any blocks underneath it in your script. In our example, it copies the **move** and the **wait** blocks. Move the copy to the bottom of your program, and click to place the blocks there. You can repeat this step several times to make the cat walk further

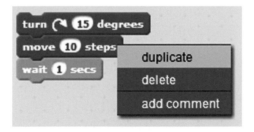

8 It's a long walk for a tiny cat, so let's make him finish his walk with a exclamation of 'Phew!' in a speech bubble. Click the **Looks** button above the Blocks Palette, and drag the **say Hello! for 2 secs** block into the Scripts Area and join it to your program. Click Hello! to edit what the cat says to Phew!

...cont'd

Right: A few blocks and one exhausted cat later, here's your first program.

9 When you start a script's commands, it's called "running" the script. To run your script, click any of the joined-up blocks in the Scripts Area. Scratch carries out all the joined-up instructions in order, starting at the top and working its way down the blocks

10 What happens if you click the script to run it again? The cat turns again and walks from where it finished last time. Eventually, it'll be walking on its head. Let's add some blocks to put it in the right starting position. Click the **Motion** button above the Blocks Palette and drag in the **point in direction 90** block and the **go to x:0 y:0** blocks. If the **go to** block has different numbers in it, edit them both to make them zero. Add these blocks to the top of your script

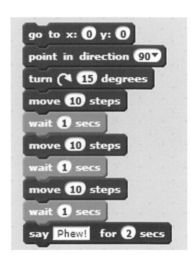

Saving your project

A Scratch project includes all the sprites, scripts and backgrounds that are used in it. It's a good idea to save your projects so you can come back to them later to reuse them or modify them.

Saving projects in Scratch 2.0

In Scratch 2.0 (web version), your work is automatically saved for you as you make changes to your project. In the top-right corner of the screen, you can see whether your latest changes have been saved. If they haven't, there will be a link here to **Save Now**.

Your project is saved with the name Untitled plus a number. You can choose a more useful name by editing the box above the Stage.

There are additional options for saving your work in the File menu, also above the Stage, see below. These include:

- **Save as a copy**: This makes a copy of your project with a new name. The previously saved version of your project is left untouched. Use this if you want to experiment with your program without losing a working version of it.

- **Download to your computer**: This enables you to save your project as a file on your computer. You can open it using the downloadable version of Scratch 2.0. If your Internet connection fails, use this option straight away to save your work!

- **Upload from your computer**: If you previously downloaded a Scratch project to your PC, or used a downloadable version of Scratch to create it, use this option to upload it to the Scratch 2.0 website.

- **Revert**: This throws away all the changes you've made to the project since you opened it this time.

Beware

You can't use projects made using Scratch 2.0 in Scratch 1.4. You can use Scratch 1.4 projects in 2.0, though.

23

Hot tip

In the downloadable version of Scratch 2.0, your work isn't automatically saved for you. Use the **Save** option in the File menu to save your work. Use the **Save As** option to save your project with a new filename, so you don't overwrite the previous version.

...cont'd

Saving and opening your project in Scratch 1.4

Click the File menu above the Blocks Palette at the top of the screen. This menu's options include:

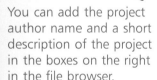

Hot tip

Click Examples on the left of the file browser to find some demo projects.

- **Open**: Opens a previously saved file.

- **Save**: Use this to save a new project, or an old project you've been editing. If you're saving a new version of a saved project, you'll replace the old saved version.

Hot tip

You can add the project author name and a short description of the project in the boxes on the right in the file browser.

- **Save as a copy**: If you want to keep the previous version of a project, use this option. It will save a new file containing your project, and leave the previous file untouched.

- **Import Project**: This enables you to open a project, and combine its sprites, scripts and backgrounds with the project that's currently open.

- **Export Sprite**: This option enables you to save a sprite as a costume you can use in other projects. You'll learn about costumes in Chapter 5.

When you save a new project or a new copy of a project, the file browser opens, as shown below. The buttons down the left are used to choose where to save your file. Click the folder name at the top (Scratch Projects in the screenshot) to choose another drive or folder, and click the up arrow beside it to go up a folder. Type the filename in the box at the bottom and click **OK**.

Don't forget

If you are using Scratch 1.4, remember to save regularly to make sure you don't lose any of your work.

Opening projects

In the downloadable version of Scratch 2.0, you open projects through the File menu at the top of the screen. The website is a bit more complicated. To find your projects there, click your username in the top-right of the screen and then click **My Stuff**. If it says "Sign in" in place of your username, click it to sign in first. The My Stuff section shows all your projects, with those you most recently edited nearer the top. Take a look at my projects in the screen below:

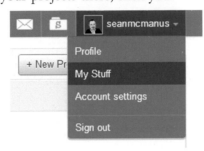

Beware

If you click the Share button on a project, it will be available for anyone to see, use and reuse. See Chapter 11 for more on sharing your projects.

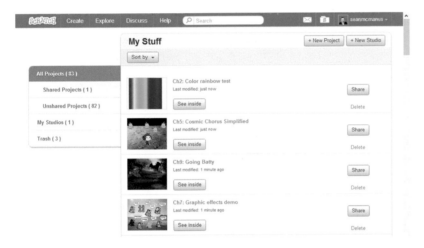

Use the scrollbar at the right edge of your browser window to find more projects and click the **Load More** button when you get to the bottom of the list. If no more projects load when you click the button, that's all of them. To open a project, click its **See inside** button.

Because projects are saved automatically, your My Stuff area quickly fills up with Untitled projects. To tidy up, delete unwanted projects by clicking their **Delete** links on the right. If you delete a project by mistake, click the Trash folder on the left, and then click the **Put back** button to recover the project.

Don't forget

In Scratch 1.4, you open projects by clicking to open the File menu at the top of the screen and then choosing Open.

Opening shared projects

You can open the projects that other people have shared on the Scratch website too. Visit the website at **http://scratch.mit.edu** and click **Explore** at the top of the screen. Use the options on the left to choose a category.

The menus in the top right enable you to sort by the most loved, most remixed and most recent, and to choose how new you want the projects to be.

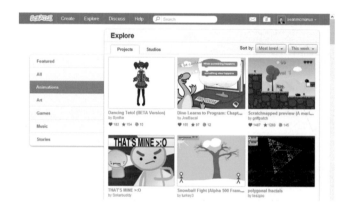

Click a project to go to its page. The instructions on the right tell you how to use the project, and you click the green flag button in the middle of the player to run it. If you like what you see, and you want to know how it was done, click the **See inside** button in the top right to go into the editor and see the scripts, sprites and backgrounds that make it work.

Beware

At the time of writing, there isn't a way to download shared projects from the website to use in Scratch 1.4.

2 Drawing with Scratch

Find your bearings on the Scratch Stage, learn how to move sprites and draw with them, and discover how loops make it easy to repeat parts of your program. You'll also make an interactive art program called Rainbow Painter.

Understanding coordinates

You can use the sprites in Scratch to draw on the Stage. It's a great way to familiarize yourself with how to move sprites, and the technique can be used to create designs that your sprites can interact with, as you'll see when we make a game in Chapter 3.

First, let's take a look at how you position sprites on the Stage. Each position on the Stage has a grid reference, similar to those used on maps. The position across the Stage horizontally is called x, and the position up or down the Stage is called y.

When you start a new project, the cat is in the middle of the Stage, and this position has the grid reference x=0 and y=0.

Here's a map of the grid references on the Stage, after I've moved the cat to the bottom left quarter of the Stage:

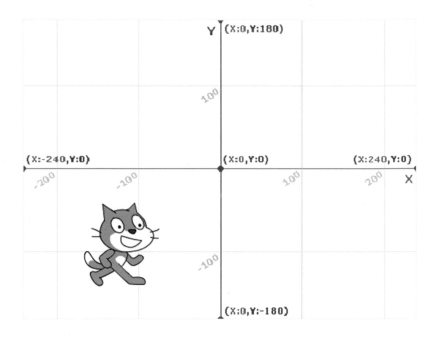

As you can see, the numbers for the y coordinate run from -180 at the bottom of the Stage, up to +180 at the top of the Stage.

The numbers for the x coordinate run from -240 at the left edge of the Stage, up to +240 at the right edge of the Stage.

Hot tip

You can click and drag your sprites around the Stage to reposition them while you're writing your programs. It's a good idea to use the "go to x:0 y:0" block to position them in the program, though, otherwise they might start off somewhere unexpected. If your sprite moves in the program, it won't be in the same position the second time the program is used. Other people can experiment with your program, too, and might move sprites around before it starts.

28

Don't forget

An easy way to remember which way around x and y should be is that "x is a cross" (and "across").

1 Click the **Motion** button above the Blocks Palette

Hot tip

To start a new project, click the File menu and then click New. If the File menu isn't showing (in Scratch 2.0), click Create in the blue menu at the top of the screen.

2 To place a sprite at a particular position on screen, use the **go to x:0 y:0** block. This block is most often used to place a sprite in its starting position. Click it and drag it into the Scripts Area

3 The numbers in the block return a sprite to the middle of the screen, but you can change the coordinates. Click the white space beside x: and enter -120. Click the white space beside y: and type -90

4 Click the block to see the cat go to its new position, in the bottom left quarter of the screen

5 Try changing the numbers in the block and clicking it to see where the cat moves around the Stage

Hot tip

You can change the numbers in the "go to x:0 y:0" block in the Blocks Palette, and Scratch sometimes changes them, too. If you're often reusing the same coordinates, that might save you time, because you can then drag the same coordinates in with your block. In this book, I'll assume this block is set to x:0 y:0 in the Blocks Palette. You can easily change the values in it, so it doesn't matter if you see something different on your screen.

Changing a sprite's position

There are several blocks you can use to change a sprite's position. To find them, click the **Motion** button above the Blocks Palette:

- **glide 1 secs to x:0 y:0**: This block makes your sprite glide across the screen to its new position. It travels in a direct and straight line. You can change the x and y coordinates in the block, and change how long the movement takes from 1 second to a value like 0.5 or 0.25 (for a faster glide), or to a bigger number for a slower one.

- **change x by 10**: This block makes your sprite move 10 positions to the right on the Stage. It doesn't affect its y position, and works independently of which way the sprite is facing. To increase how far the sprite moves, use a bigger number.

- **change x by -10**: To make your sprite move left, edit the value in the **change x by** block to make it a negative number. To make the sprite move further, use a bigger negative number.

- **change y by 10**: This block makes your sprite move 10 positions up the Stage. It doesn't affect its horizontal position, and also works independently of which way the sprite is facing. Change the 10 to a bigger number for a bigger movement.

- **change y by -10**: Similar to the way you make a sprite move left, you can make a sprite move down the screen by changing the 10 in the **change y by** block to a negative number. For a bigger movement, use a bigger negative number.

- **set x to 0**: This block changes your sprite's horizontal position to a specific number without affecting its vertical position.

- **set y to 0**: This block changes your sprite's vertical position to a specific number without affecting its horizontal position.

Using the pen

The pen in Scratch enables a sprite to draw a line as it moves around the Stage. The blocks are:

- **clear**: This clears all the drawing on the Stage, but doesn't disturb the background or any sprites.

- **pen down**: This is like putting the pen down on a piece of paper. After you use this, your sprite leaves a line wherever it goes.

- **pen up**: This block stops your sprite from drawing as it moves. Sprites start with the pen up, so they won't leave a line unless you put the pen down.

- **set pen color to [color]**: This block enables you to use a pipette to choose which color you'd like to use with the pen. Click the box of color inside the block and then click a color somewhere else on the screen to use it. In Scratch 1.4, you're also shown a palette to choose colors from (see below).

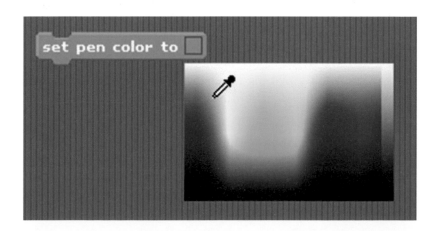

...cont'd

- **change pen color by 10**: Each color has a number, and the colors are arranged like a rainbow. Use this block to change the pen color to a higher number. Using a negative number, will change the pen color to a lower number.

- **set pen color to 0**:
  You can also set the color to a specific number, between 0 and 200. If you use higher numbers, they do work, but the same colors repeat. Color 350 is the same as 150, for example. To the right, you can see the pen colors from 0 on the left to 200 on the right.

- **set pen shade to 50**: You can change how bright or dark the color you use is. The starting value is 50, and the range of numbers goes from 0 to 100. Lower numbers darken the color, with 0 being black. Higher numbers lighten the color, with 100 being white. If you use numbers above 100, they do work, but the scale reverses every 100 numbers, so numbers from 101 to 200 go from light to dark, and from 201 to 300 go from dark to light again.

- **change pen shade by 10**: Use this block to change the shade, relative to its current value. Use a positive or negative number, depending on whether you want the number of the pen shade to go up or down.

- **change pen size by 1**: This block increases the pen size. Use a negative number to decrease it.

- **set pen size to 1**: Use this block to set the pen size to a specific width. Anything larger than 5 leaves a thick line. The maximum size is 255, but this is too big to be useful often.

- **stamp**: This block prints a copy of the sprite on the Stage, so when the sprite moves on, it will leave a picture of itself behind. It's just a picture of the sprite, not a copy of the sprite that you can control. In Chapter 4, you'll learn how to clone and duplicate sprites, so you can control the copies.

Don't forget

The Pen blocks are colored dark green, and you show them in the Blocks Palette by clicking the Pen button above it.

Drawing a house in Scratch

You can use what you've learned about moving sprites and the pen to draw pictures on the Stage. Follow these steps to draw a house:

1 Change the background to xy-grid, which puts a grid onto the Stage to help you work out coordinates. You can find it in the Other category in Scratch 2.0, and it's in the top folder with all the other background folders in Scratch 1.4

2 Click your cat sprite, and click the **Scripts** tab to open the Scripts Area

3 There's a potential pitfall here: if the pen is down, then the sprite will draw a line you don't want as it moves into place. To fix that, lift the pen before moving the sprite. Click the **Pen** button above the Blocks Palette and drag the **clear** and **pen up** blocks into the top of your script

4 Click the **Motion** button above the Blocks Palette and drag in the **go to x:0 y:0** block. Change the numbers in it to x:-100 y:-100, so it puts the sprite in the right starting position

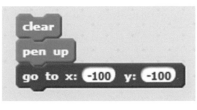

5 Next, we should get ready to draw. Use **pen down** to start drawing, and set the pen color and size to something that will stand out from the grid pattern. Add these blocks to the bottom of your script

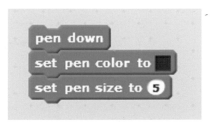

Hot tip

The picture is drawn almost instantly. To slow it down so you can see what's happening, add some "wait" blocks between the movement blocks. You can find the "wait" block among the Control blocks.

33

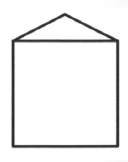

Above: The house we're drawing.

...cont'd

6 Our sprite is now positioned in the bottom left corner of our house. To draw the square, move the sprite up (increasing the y coordinate), right (increasing the x coordinate), down (decreasing the y coordinate), and left (decreasing the x coordinate). Each line has a length of 200, so the sprite ends where it started. Click the **Motion** button above the Blocks Palette and add these blocks to your script

Hot tip

Why not see if you can add windows and a door? Remember to lift the pen before repositioning the pen inside the square.

7 To draw the roof, we need to move the cat to the top left corner of the house first. If we change the x position and y position separately, we'll leave two

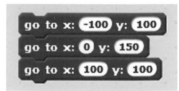

lines in an L shape. To draw a straight diagonal line, we use the **go to x:0 y:0 block** to move to the tip of the roof, and use it again to move to the right corner of the house. Drag in these blocks

8 Click your script to run it, and you should see the scene below on the Stage

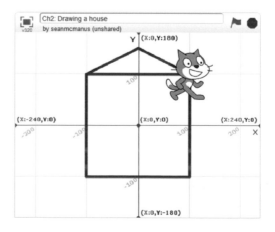

Above: the finished program

Using directions to move

As you saw last chapter, there is another way you can move sprites in Scratch, which is to point them in a particular direction and then move them forwards in that direction. Here are the blocks you use for that:

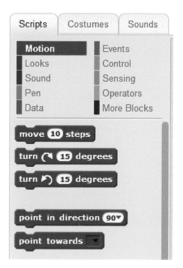

- **move 10 steps**: This moves your sprite forwards. In the case of the cat, this usually means the direction it's facing. You can change the number of steps, and a negative number makes the sprite go backwards.

- **turn clockwise 15 degrees**: This rotates your sprite clockwise by 15 degrees. You can change the number of degrees. You can use a negative number to turn the other way, but you will rarely need to, because of the next block.

- **turn anti-clockwise 15 degrees**: This block turns your sprite in the other direction.

- **point towards**: This block is used to point a sprite towards another sprite, or the mouse pointer.

- **point in direction 90**: This makes your sprite point in a particular direction. The direction numbers go from -179 to 180. There is a menu in the block you can click to choose one of the most common directions: right (90), left (-90), up (0), or down (180). You can also type in a number of your choice.

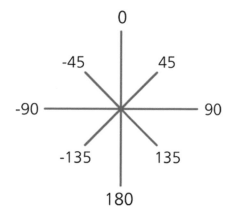

Don't forget

Which is better? Moving using coordinates, or using directions? There's no right answer to that: it depends on your program. Part of the art of programming is to choose the best approach for each program you write. We'll use both methods in this book, sometimes in the same program.

Hot tip

When you turn your sprite, Scratch makes sure the numbers make sense automatically. For example, when the direction is 180 (down) and you rotate clockwise by 90 degrees, Scratch turns the resulting direction into -90 (left) instead of 270, which would be mathematically correct, but is outside the range of directions Scratch uses.

Keeping sprites upright

One of the problems with rotating sprites is that it can look strange, even in the context of a game. When you rotate the cat to move up (direction 0), it looks like it's climbing the walls:

Worse still, when its direction is set to left (-90), the cat looks like it's walking on its head.

To avoid this problem, you can change the rotation style of the sprite. There are three styles to choose from:

- **all around**: This is the "normal" setting, that makes the sprite turn all the way around depending on its direction, and can make the sprite appear to defy logic and gravity. The sprite turns to face the direction it will move in.

- **left-right:** This keeps your sprite's feet on the ground and makes it face either left or right, but never up or down or at an angle. You can move the sprite in any direction, but it will always face right or left.

- **don't rotate**: This stops the sprite from visibly changing when its direction changes. You can still change its direction and move it in that direction, but the sprite will always look exactly the same.

Setting rotation style in Scratch 2.0

There is a new block in Scratch 2.0 called **set rotation style**. Click the **Motion** button above the Blocks Palette and then use the scrollbar (on the right edge of the Blocks Palette) to find this block near the bottom.

You can rotate your sprite without using blocks if you need a quick fix. In Scratch 2.0, use the circle icon beside the direction in the information panel. In Scratch 1.4, use the picture of your sprite above the Scripts Area. In both cases, click and drag in a circle to rotate the sprite.

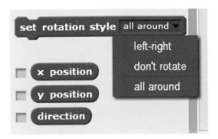

You can also change the rotation style of the sprite by clicking the sprite in the Sprite List and then clicking the **i** (for information) button in the corner of it. Click one of the three rotation style options to select it, and then click the back arrow (white triangle on blue circle) in the top-left of the information panel to close it.

Setting rotation style in Scratch 1.4

To change the rotation style in Scratch 1.4, click the sprite in the Sprite List to select it (if necessary), and then click one of the three buttons above the Scripts Area. The buttons are on the left of the picture of your sprite. The first button changes the rotation style to all around, the second button to left-right, and the third button turns off rotation.

Above: The information button on the cat sprite.

Drawing using directions

You can draw pictures by moving the sprite with directions too. Earlier in this chapter, you saw how to draw a house by moving the cat to specific points on the Stage.

You can also use directions to achieve the same effect. Here's a program to draw a square:

Don't forget

You can duplicate blocks by right-clicking them (See Chapter 1).

38

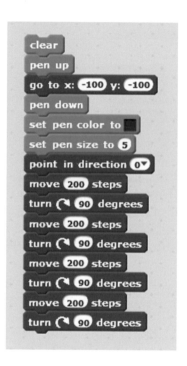

- The first six blocks are the same as we used when drawing the house, and just prepare our sprite for drawing.

- The next block turns it to point up the screen.

- Then we move it forwards 200 steps, which draws a line up the screen.

- We rotate 90 degrees right (so the sprite is facing right), move it again to draw the top of the square.

- Then we make two more turns and lines.

There's a lot of repetition in there: we have included the same two instructions four times in a row. It works, but it's laborious to create and hard to read. Luckily, there is a better solution.

Making shapes using Repeat

In our square drawing program, it would be far simpler to tell the program to go forward and turn right four times, than it is to list out every turn and movement.

The **repeat 10** block makes this possible. It is one of the Control blocks, which determine whether and how often things happen in a program. It's shaped like a bracket, and you put the blocks you want to repeat inside it. You change the number in the block's frame to say how often you want it to repeat the blocks inside.

Here is how you can use the **repeat 10** block to draw a square:

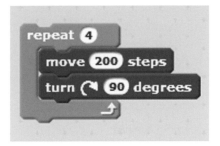

The blocks to move and turn sit inside the **repeat** block's bracket, and the **repeat** block is set to repeat them four times.

Repeating sections of program like this are often called loops. It's easier to see what's happening in this program than it was when we had so many drawing instructions, and it's easier to modify the program too.

What if you decide you need a hexagon instead of a square? You can just increase the number of times the sprite moves and turns, from 4 to 6 (for the 6 sides and angles), and also change the size of the turn to 60 degrees.

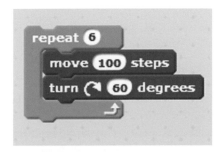

Hot tip

You can modify this loop to draw any shape with sides of the same length. To work out the angle of the turn, divide 360 by the number of sides. To alter the size of the shape, change the distance the sprite moves for each line.

Hot tip

For best results, add these example loops after the first six blocks from the previous example that set up the Stage.

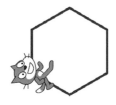

Above: The square becomes a hexagon with a small change to the loop.

Putting loops inside loops

Beware

Take care with where you put your blocks. For example, if you put the block to change the pen color inside the inner "repeat" block that draws the hexagon, the pen color will change with each line. That doesn't matter so much with abstract demonstrations like this, but it can cause huge problems in more elaborate programs.

You can put **repeat** blocks inside each other, for example if you want to draw lots of hexagons, each one slightly offset from the previous one. Start a new project and try making this program. It creates a pattern of overlapping hexagons as shown below.

The first few blocks set the sprite up, facing right, in the middle of the Stage. Then we set the pen up, by clearing any previous digital doodles, putting the pen down and setting the pen size.

After that, we have the first of our loops, which will repeat 72 times. If you look inside it, you can see the first thing it does is use another loop which repeats 6 times to draw a hexagon.

After that loop has finished and the hexagon is drawn, the pen color is changed and the sprite is turned by 5 degrees. Then the process repeats, with another hexagon drawn, the color changed and the sprite rotated until 72 hexagons are on screen.

Hot tip

A loop inside a loop is called a nested loop.

Hot tip

The outer loop repeats 72 times because it turns 5 degrees each time. 72 times 5 degrees makes 360 degrees, a full circle.

Creating Rainbow Painter

To close this chapter, here's a simple art program called Rainbow Painter that enables you to paint with a striped pen across the starry night sky. It shows you how simple it can be to make a program that interacts with the user. Once you've written it, you can use this program to make your own digital designs:

1 Start a new project, and change the background to stars. It's in the Space theme in Scratch 2.0 and the Nature folder in Scratch 1.4

2 Click the cat in the Sprite List and click the **Scripts** tab to open the Scripts Area

3 It's possible to hide a sprite, so it's not shown on the screen but it can still move around and draw on the Stage. We'll use a hidden sprite that follows the mouse pointer to draw on the Stage. You can use the cat sprite that stars in every new project for this. Click the **Looks** button above the Blocks Palette to find the **hide** block

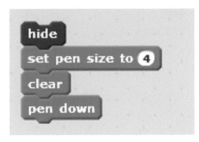

4 Drag in the following blocks to set up the program

5 As well as the **repeat** block, there is a **forever** block which repeats whatever is inside it endlessly. It's another Control block, so click the **Control** button above the Blocks Palette to find it

6 Drag it in and join it to the program so far

Don't forget

The color of the blocks provides a hint about where you can find them in the Blocks Palette. To find the green blocks, click the green button above the Blocks Palette.

Hot tip

Notice that there's no slot on the bottom of the "forever" block for other blocks to lock into. That's because a forever loop never ends, so any blocks underneath it would never be used.

...cont'd

7 Drag in the Motion block **go to** and click the menu in it to choose the mouse-pointer. This moves your invisible sprite to the mouse pointer. As you move the mouse, the sprite will keep moving to the mouse's new position and will leave a line behind it

8 Drag in the block to change the pen color by 10, so the color is continuously changing

When you run the program and move your mouse pointer over the Stage, you'll leave a rainbow colored line. Below you can see a face drawn using Rainbow Painter.

42

Above: The final program looks like this.

3 Spiral Rider

Learn how to make your first game, including using the green flag to start scripts, using variables to store a number, moving a sprite with the keyboard, and letting Scratch make simple decisions about which blocks should run.

Introducing Spiral Rider

Poor Freddy Fish has bought a new T-shirt and the tag in the back is really itching. Chris the Crab has claws that could clip the tag off, if only the pair could meet up. Chris has crawled through a maze of passages in the rock. Can you help Freddy get there?

Behind this silly premise lies a game that will use what you have already learned about Scratch and take it further to help you make your first real game. You'll learn:

- How to keep track of a number, so you can make a square spiral with ever decreasing line lengths;

- How to use multiple sprites, and use the green flag to synchronize them;

- How to move sprites with the keyboard;

- How to make a sprite move automatically;

- How to detect when a sprite hits something; and

- How the graphic effects can be used on the background.

In this game, you control the fish using the cursor keys, and must turn at the right time on each corner to navigate the spiral successfully. If you hit the spiral, it's game over.

Using the green flag

So far we've started our programs by just clicking the stack of blocks we want to run. There are a few problems with this:

- When someone else uses the program, they might not know which stack of blocks they should run first.

- It's not user-friendly. Someone who wants to just play your game should be able to do so without having to look at its blocks.

- It's difficult to synchronize different sprites to start at the same time.

Scratch provides a simple solution to problems like this with the green flag, a button above the Stage used to start programs. Scripts on different sprites can detect when that button is clicked, and can then start at the same time.

People using Scratch programs know how to start programs using the green flag too. When you share programs through the Scratch website, they're shown with a prominent green flag button in the middle of the Stage, like a play button on a video.

There is a block you can use at the top of your stack of blocks to start them when the green flag is clicked:

It has a curved top because no other blocks can connect to the top of it: it is always the first block in its stack. Blocks like this are called hat blocks.

This block is categorized differently in the two versions of Scratch:

- In Scratch 2.0 it's a brown Events block. Events blocks are used for detecting when things happen, such as buttons being clicked. The Events category is new in Scratch 2.0.

- In Scratch 1.4, it's a yellow Control block. In Scratch 1.4, Events blocks and Control blocks are mixed in together.

Don't forget

This block has a different color in Scratch 2.0 and Scratch 1.4. In my screenshots, I'll use Scratch 2.0, so remember where to find this block if you're using a Raspberry Pi.

Hot tip

You can still click a stack of blocks to run them, even if there is a "when green flag clicked" block at the top of them, and this can be useful for testing scripts.

Above: When you share a program on the Scratch website, it has a big green flag button so users know how to start it.

Creating variables

We're going to draw our spiral starting at the outside and working our way inwards. The way we draw a spiral is similar to how we draw a square: we draw a line, turn 90 degrees and repeat until we reach the middle. The big difference is that the lines get shorter as we move towards the middle.

That means we need a way to remember the length of the line, and to shorten it. Variables are used in Scratch (and other programming languages) to store information we want to remember, so we can reuse it and change it. You could use a variable to keep track of a score, the number of lives left, the player's name, or the right answer in a word guessing game.

Start a new project, and click on the cat sprite, which we will use to draw our spiral. Let's make a variable to store the length of the lines in the spiral:

 In Scratch 2.0 (left, below), the blocks for variables are categorized as Data blocks, so click **Data** at the top of the Blocks Palette. In Scratch 1.4 (right, below), the blocks are categorized as Variables blocks, so click **Variables** at the top of the Blocks Palette

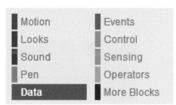 

Don't forget

They're called variables because the information they store (their values) can vary. Their name stays the same though. The number in the score variable might change, for example, but the name of the variable will stay *score*.

2 Click the **Make a Variable** button in the Blocks Palette. A pop-up box appears, like this

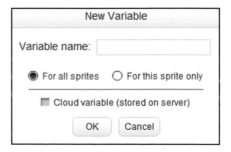

3 The first thing we need to do is name our variable. You can use spaces in Scratch variable names. Type **line length** into the box, but don't press Enter yet

4 When you make a variable, you can choose whether it can be used by all sprites or just the current sprite. You can't change this later, so pause for thought here. We'll make this variable for this sprite only, because other sprites don't need it and shouldn't use it

5 In Scratch 2.0, you can make a cloud variable. This means the variable is shared between everyone using your program on the Scratch website. If 10 people play your game, for example, they could all see (and change) the same high score number if it's in a cloud variable. Leave the Cloud variable box unticked. (For more on cloud variables, see Chapter 8)

6 Click the **OK** button

7 The Blocks Palette now contains some new blocks for managing your variable, shown below. The block with rounded ends has a tickbox beside it. When ticked, it shows your variable and its value on the Stage. We don't need that for this variable, so untick it. The blocks to set and change the variable values have menus in them that you can use to choose which variable you'd like to change, and a box where you can type a number or some text

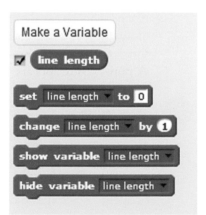

Hot tip

If a variable is set up for just one sprite, other sprites can't use its value or change its value. That stops them causing errors by interfering with a variable they shouldn't, so it's considered a good idea where possible.

Don't forget

Keep variable names short but meaningful so you can easily understand your program. A good variable name is something like *alien speed*.

Beware

Two sprites can have variables with the same name that work completely independently. This happens, for example, if you give a sprite a variable for that sprite only, and then duplicate that sprite. See duplication in Chapter 4.

Drawing a spiral

We'll use our new variable to draw a spiral on the Stage. Follow these steps to add the blocks needed to your cat sprite:

1 Above the Blocks Palette, click the **Events** button in Scratch 2.0, or the **Control** button in Scratch 1.4. Drag the **when green flag clicked** block into the Scripts Area to start your script

2 It looks best if our spiral seems to magically appear from nowhere, so let's make the cat invisible. Click the **Looks** button above the Blocks Palette and add the **hide** block to your stack

3 To put our cat in its starting position (the top left of the screen), click the **Motion** button above the Blocks Palette and drag the **go to x:0 y:0** and **point in direction 90** blocks into your stack. Change the values in the **go to** block to x: -180 and y: 170 by clicking and editing the numbers

4 Click **Pen** above the Blocks Palette, and drag in these blocks. This clears the screen of any drawing that's already there, and gets the pen ready to draw this time

5 We need to set the starting value of our *line length* variable. I've chosen 340, because the height of the Stage is 360, so a maximum spiral height of 340 fits comfortably. Click the **Data** button above the Blocks Palette in Scratch 2.0, or the **Variables** button in Scratch 1.4. Drag the block **set line length to 0** into your script. Then click the box in the block and edit the number 0 to 340

6 Our spiral uses two loops, one inside the other. The inner loop draws a line, turns 90 degrees and then does the same again, so it repeats its blocks twice in total. The line length is then shortened, and the process repeats, six times in total. In the picture below, I've changed the pen color each time the line length is shortened. Lines of the same color are drawn by the same inner loop

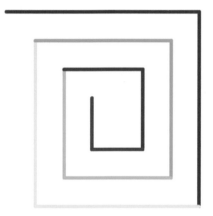

Hot tip

You can see the complete program for drawing a spiral on the next page.

7 Click the **Control** button above the Blocks Palette and drag the **repeat 10** block into your stack. Drag another **repeat 10** block in, and set the outer loop to repeat six times, and the inner loop to repeat twice

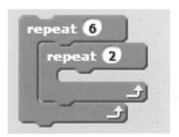

8 Click the **Motion** button above the Blocks Palette, and drag in **move 10 steps** and **turn clockwise 15 degrees**. Change the number in the **turn** block to 90 degrees

...cont'd

⁹ You can use a variable in place of a number. Instead of moving 10 steps, or any other fixed number, we want to move the same number as we've stored in our *line length* variable. To do this, we can replace the number in the **move** block with the variable name. Click the **Data** or **Variables** button above the Blocks Palette, and drag the rounded block containing the *line length* variable name into the **move 10 steps** block

Hot tip

The shapes of the blocks give you a hint how they can be used. The "move 10 steps" block has a rounded hole, and the block for the *line length* variable has rounded edges, so you can easily see that one fits inside the other.

¹⁰ After the inner loop ends, and an L shape has been drawn, we want to shorten the length of the lines. Drag in the Data or Variables block **change line length by 1**. Make sure it joins underneath the inner **repeat** block, and doesn't go inside its bracket. Change the number in it to -50

¹¹ Click the green flag button above the Stage to see your spiral appear!

You can see our finished script to the right

Changing the background

We have our spiral, but we can make our game look much more interesting by adding in an underwater background:

1 Add one of the underwater backgrounds to your project. Scratch 2.0 has three to choose from in its Underwater theme. Scratch 1.4 has just the one, in the Nature folder

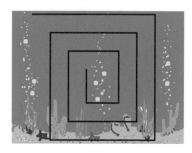

Hot tip

The ghost graphic effect uses a number from 0 to 100, which is a percentage. When the ghost effect on the background is at 100%, the background is invisible.

2 The background I've chosen is quite vibrant, and makes it hard to see what's going on in the game. We can tone it down using a graphic effect. To do that, we will add blocks to the Stage. Click the Stage icon beside the Sprite List. Open the Scripts Area by clicking the **Scripts** tab above the Blocks Palette in Scratch 2.0 or above the Scripts Area in Scratch 1.4

3 Click the **Events** button (Scratch 2.0) or **Control** button (Scratch 1.4) above the Blocks Palette. Drag the **when green flag clicked** block into the Scripts Area

4 Click the **Looks** button above the Blocks Palette. Drag in the block **set color effect to 0** and join it to **when green flag clicked**

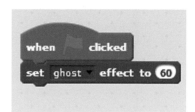

Hot tip

You can also apply the graphic effects to sprites, as you'll see later on. The ghost effect makes sprites transparent.

5 In the **set effect** block, click the menu to choose the ghost effect. Change the number in the block to 60

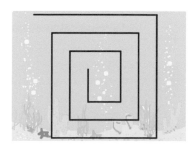

6 When you click the green flag, the background lightens (see right)

Adding sprites

Our game will use three sprites: the invisible cat sprite, which draws the spiral, Freddy the Fish, and Chris the Crab. The way you add sprites is different in Scratch 2.0 and Scratch 1.4.

Adding sprites in Scratch 2.0

1 Between the Sprite List and the Stage is a row of buttons for making new sprites. You can choose a sprite from the library, paint a new sprite (see Chapter 4), upload a sprite from a file if you have a picture you've already made, or use a webcam to take a photo to use as a sprite. Click to choose a sprite from the library

2 The Sprite Library opens, and looks similar to the library of backgrounds you used previously. You can click categories and themes on the left to browse the different sprites available. Click the Animals category, click the Crab and then click **OK**

3 Repeat the process, but this time select the sprite Fish1, which is also in the Animals category. Use the scrollbar on the right of the Sprite Library to see more sprites

Hot tip

There are two types of sprites in Scratch 2.0: vectors and bitmaps. Vectors look better when you change their size. When you have a choice, pick a vector over a bitmap.

Hot tip

You can also double click a sprite in the Sprite Library to open it.

Adding sprites in Scratch 1.4

1 Above the Sprite List are three buttons you can use to add a new sprite. From the left, they enable you to paint a new sprite (see Chapter 4), choose a new sprite from a file, or get a surprise sprite. Click the middle button to get a sprite from a file

2 The file browser opens, ready for you to browse the sprites supplied

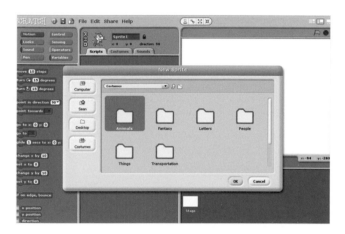

Hot tip

In the file browser, you can use the buttons on the left to go to your computer or Desktop to find your own pictures to use as sprites in Scratch.

53

3 Double click on the Animals folder and use the scrollbar to find crab1-a. Click it and then click **OK**

Hot tip

The "surprise sprite" button can give you some great ideas for games you could make, by bringing together all kinds of different people, creatures and things!

4 Repeat the process, but this time select the sprite fish2, which is also in the Animals category

Animating the crab

When the game starts, we need to position the crab in the middle of the spiral and set its size. To make it look more lifelike, we can make it bob from side to side during the game. Follow these steps to create the script for the crab:

1 Click the crab in the Sprite List to make sure you're adding your script to the right sprite

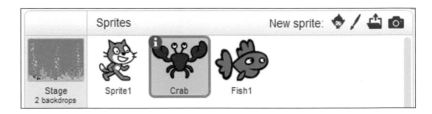

2 Click the **Events** button (Scratch 2.0) or **Control** button (Scratch 1.4) above the Blocks Palette. Drag the **when green flag clicked** block into the Scripts Area to start your script

3 Click the **Motion** button above the Blocks Palette and drag the **go to x:0 y:0** block

4 Change the values in the **go to** block to x: 10 and y: -15 by clicking and editing the numbers

5 Click the **Looks** button above the Blocks Palette and drag the **set size to 100%** block

6 Click the number in the block and change it to 30. The choice of 30% wasn't scientific: I arrived at it through trial and error, after trying several different numbers. I wanted the crab to be as big as possible, but still fit in the middle of the spiral

7 Check your script so far (right)

when clicked
go to x: 10 y: -15
set size to 30 %

8   Click the **Control** button above the Blocks Palette and drag the **forever** block into your stack. We'll use this to make our crab hop left and right all the time the game is playing

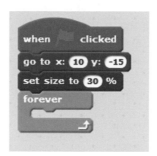

9   Drag two **wait 1 secs** blocks into the bracket of the **forever** block, so they're joined to each other

10   Click the **Motion** button above the Blocks Palette, and drag in two **change x by 10** blocks. Position one after each of the **wait 1 secs** blocks. Click the number 10 in the first **change x by** block and change it to 2. Change the number in the other one to -2

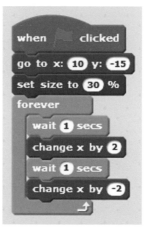

Hot tip

You don't have to add blocks in the order they will be used by the program. We added two "wait" blocks in one go, and then two "change x" blocks in one go. That saved time switching between the categories in the Blocks Palette.

11   Test it works by clicking the green flag button above the Stage. You can click and drag the fish out of the way

Enabling keyboard control

There are a couple of different techniques you can use to make a sprite move in a game, as you'll see in other projects in this book. For this game, we'll make the fish swim all the time, so players have to steer it to stop it hitting the spiral. When a player presses one of the cursor keys, we'll change Freddy's direction.

There is a block you can use to start a script when a particular key is pressed on the keyboard. In Scratch 2.0, this is an Events block and in Scratch 1.4, it is a Control block:

 Click the fish in the Sprite List to make sure you're adding your script to the right sprite

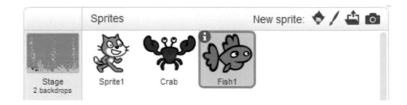

 Don't forget

The "when space key pressed" block is a brown Events block in Scratch 2.0, but it's a yellow Control block in Scratch 1.4.

2 In Scratch 2.0 (left, below), click the **Events** button above the Blocks Palette. In Scratch 1.4 (right, below), click the **Control** button above the Blocks Palette

3 Drag the **when space key pressed** block into the Scripts Area. Like the **when green flag clicked** block, this is a hat block and has a curved top because nothing can go above it. This block always starts off the stack of blocks it is connected to

4 Click the menu in this block, and you can choose which key you want to detect. Click **up arrow**

5 Click the **Motion** button above the Blocks Palette. Drag in the **point in direction 90** block, and join it to your **when up arrow key pressed** block. Click the direction menu to open it and then click **(0) up**

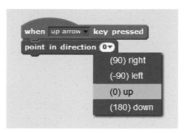

Hot tip

To save time switching between different parts of the Blocks Palette, you could drag in four "when space key pressed" blocks, drag in four "point in direction" blocks, and then organize them in the Scripts Area.

57

6 Repeat these steps to detect the down, left and right arrow keys, and to change the direction of the fish when they're pressed. It's okay to have several different and unconnected scripts for a sprite. Here's what the finished movement key detection scripts should look like

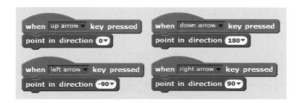

7 Press the cursor keys to check the fish changes direction. Note that it won't actually move around the screen yet

Making the fish move

Our script for the fish puts it in the starting position (the bottom left of the screen), points it in the right direction (up), and adjusts its size so it can fit in the spiral. The script then keeps it moving until it hits either the spiral or the crab. If it hits the spiral, we display a message that says "Ouch". Otherwise, we display a happy message because the player has reached the crab.

Here's how you make the script for the fish:

1 Click the fish in the Sprite List to make sure you're adding your scripts to the right sprite

2 The first few blocks will be familiar to you by now, so drag them into the Scripts Area and change the values in them. The fish should start at x:-180 y:-140, pointing in direction 0 (up), and with a size of 24%

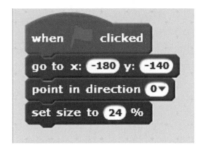

3 To keep the fish moving until it hits something, you use the **repeat until** block. It's a Control block. Drag it in and join it to your script

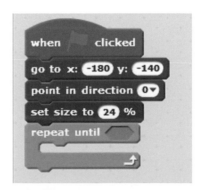

4 Inside the bracket of the **repeat until** block, add a **move 10 steps** block, and change the number in it to 4. This is all you need inside the **repeat until** bracket. Remember you've added four other scripts to change the fish's direction when a key is pressed

5 The **repeat until** block has a diamond-shaped hole in it. This is where you tell Scratch that you want it to repeat the loop until the fish hits the spiral or the crab. Click the **Operators** button above the Blocks Palette, and drag the **or** block into the diamond shaped hole

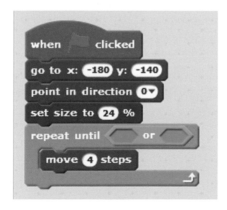

Hot tip

To speed the game up, change the number 4 in the "move 4 steps" block to a higher number.

Hot tip

The "or" Operator block is used because we want to move the fish until it hits the crab *or* the spiral. There is another Operator block you can use to check whether two things are both true. If we had used the "and" block instead of the "or" block, the fish would move until it was touching both the spiral and the crab.

6 To see whether the fish has hit the spiral or the crab, you use two Sensing blocks. Click the **Sensing** button above the Scripts Area. Drag the **touching?** block and drop it onto the left of the green block. The **touching?** block is used for checking whether a sprite is touching another object, such as another sprite or the mouse pointer. Click the menu in it, and select Crab (in Scratch 2.0) or Sprite2 in Scratch 1.4. Both refer to the crab, but the two versions of Scratch use different names for the sprites you added

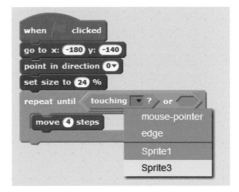

7 Drag the **touching color?** block into the other side of the **or** block. Click the square of color inside your **touching color?** block, and then click your spiral on the Stage. This will put the color of your spiral into the block

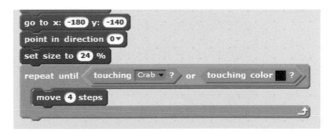

8 As always, test it works! Click the green flag button above the Stage. You should now find you can move the fish around and it'll keep moving until it hits either the spiral or the crab

Adding Game Over messages

There are two ways the game can end: the fish is touching the crab (which means the player won), or the fish is touching the color of the spiral, which means they crashed. We can use an **if... then... else** block to display a different message, depending on how the game ended:

1 The **if... then... else** block is a Control block. Drag it into the Scripts Area and join it to the bottom of your **repeat until** block

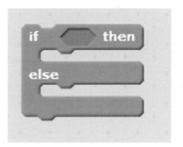

Beware

The "if... then... else" block is just called "if... else" in Scratch 1.4. It does exactly the same job, but it doesn't have the word "then" on it.

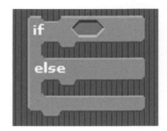

61

2 Right-click the **touching color?** block you used in your **repeat until** block. A menu opens. Choose **duplicate**

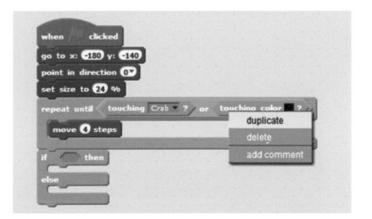

3 As you move the mouse, a copy of the **touching color?** block will move with it. Click the mouse button to drop the block into the diamond-shaped hole of the **if... then... else** block

...cont'd

4 Click the **Looks** button above the Blocks Palette. Drag a **say Hello! for 2 secs** block into both of the brackets in your **if... then... else** block

5 This **say** block displays a message in a speech bubble. After the time specified (2 seconds is the standard), it disappears again. Click the "Hello!" text in the first **say** block, and change it to "Ouch!". Change the text in the second **say** block to "Hurrah! You won!". The way the **if... then... else** block works is that it checks whether something is true, and if it is, it runs the blocks in its first bracket, and otherwise it runs the blocks in

its second bracket. We're checking whether the fish has hit the spiral, so if it has, the first **say** block will display the message for losing the game. If the fish isn't touching the spiral, it must be touching the crab, so the program shows the congratulations message

6 Your final script looks like this

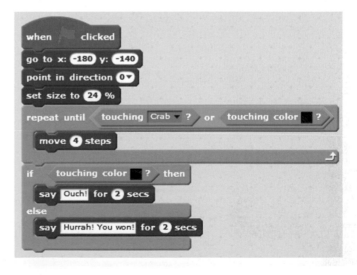

4 Super Dodgeball

In this chapter, you'll make a game where you have to dodge bouncing balls and collect ice creams. As you build the game, you'll learn a new way to move sprites, how to make random numbers and use them to add suspense to a game, how to paint your own sprites, and how to copy and clone sprites. The chapter concludes with tips for changing the speed of the game.

Introducing Super Dodgeball

It can be hard to relax at the seaside with so many other people around, playing games and getting in the way. In Super Dodgeball, you have to avoid all the beachballs bouncing around.

Each time a ball hits you, your strength is sapped. Your energy is shown with a semi-transparent picture of your cat character, which shrinks as your strength decreases.

You score by collecting ice creams which pop up on the screen, but they soon disappear again if you're not quick enough. Ice cream also gives you a small dose of energy, to help you recover from being hit by the beachballs.

In this chapter, you'll learn how to:

- Move sprites in a new way, under keyboard control

- Design your own sprites

- Add randomness to your game

- Copy sprites

- Add sound effects

- Adjust the game's difficulty

Beware

To get this game working, you'll need to do some things differently in Scratch 1.4 to Scratch 2.0, but I'll tell you about those as you make your way through the chapter.

Setting up the variables

We'll use two variables in this game: one to keep track of the player's score, and one to keep track of the player's percentage strength remaining:

1 Click the **Data** button (Scratch 2.0) or the **Variables** button (Scratch 1.4) above the Blocks Palette

Don't forget

It's a new project, so start with a clean slate. Use the File menu and choose New or click the Create button at the top of the screen to start afresh!

2 Click the **Make a Variable** button in the Blocks Palette

Make a Variable

3 Type **score** into the Variable name box. The standard options are correct for this variable (make the variable for all sprites, and don't make it a cloud variable). That means you can just press Enter or click the **OK** button

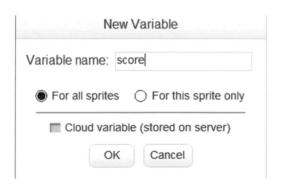

New Variable

Variable name: score

● For all sprites   ○ For this sprite only

☐ Cloud variable (stored on server)

OK   Cancel

Don't forget

Cloud variables are explained in Chapter 8, and are only available in Scratch 2.0.

4 Repeat the process, but this time enter the name **strength** to create the *strength* variable

...cont'd

5 When you make variables, reporting boxes are added to the Stage to display their values. They appear in the top left corner, but you can move them. Click the *score* box and drag it to the top right corner, and release the mouse button to position it there. We won't use the *strength* box, so you can leave that where it is

6 In the Blocks Palette, there are rounded blocks for each of your variables. The tickbox beside them decides whether the variable should be shown on the Stage. We'll show the player's strength using our energy meter instead of the variable box on the Stage, so untick the box beside the *strength* variable

7 Displaying the variable boxes on the Stage can noticeably slow down your Scratch programs on the Raspberry Pi. For that reason, if you're using a Raspberry Pi, untick the box beside the *score* variable. It would be ideal to display it all the time, but we can make the game faster and more fun by just showing it at the end of the game

Hot tip

There's a lot of work going on to speed up Scratch on the Raspberry Pi, so it's worth testing the game to see whether you can display the score on screen all the time using the latest software update.

Preparing for the game start

Before you start bouncing balls and designing your dream ice cream, there are a few other things you need to prepare:

1 When the game starts, we need to position and size the cat correctly. Above the Blocks Palette, click the **Events** button in Scratch 2.0, or the **Control** button in Scratch 1.4. Drag the **when green flag clicked** block into the Scripts Area

2 Click the **Looks** button above the Blocks Palette and drag in the **set size to 100%** block. Change the number in it to 50. Shrinking the cat makes it easier to dodge the beachballs, which makes the game more playable

3 Click the **Motion** button. Drag in the **go to x:0 y:0** block. This ensures the cat starts in the middle of the Stage

4 Click the **Data** button (in Scratch 2.0) or the **Variables** button (in Scratch 1.4) above the Blocks Palette. Drag in the **set score to 0** block. This ensures the score starts at zero each time the game is played

5 Unless you're using a Raspberry Pi, your script is below (left). If you are using a Raspberry Pi, drag in the **hide variable score** block. Hiding the variable on the Stage during the game helps speed it up (below right)

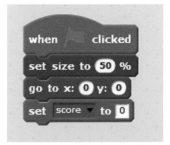 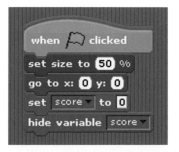

Beware

You might think that some of these blocks are unnecessary because the cat's already in the middle and the score's already zero. But what happens when someone plays twice? The second time around, the score and cat position will carry on from the first game unless you reset them.

Using coordinates to move

Last chapter, you learned how to use directions to move a sprite under keyboard control. Spiral Rider used a loop to move the sprite continuously, and used the controls to change its direction.

For this game, we'll use a different technique. Each time a cursor key is pressed, the program will change the sprite's x or y coordinate slightly, making the sprite appear to move.

This is how to use this technique:

- To go right, change the x coordinate by a positive number

- To go left, change the x coordinate by a negative number

- To go up, change the y coordinate by a positive number

- To do down, change the y coordinate by a negative number

Follow these steps to add the player's movements:

1 Click the **Control** button above the Blocks Palette

2 Drag the **forever** block into your cat's script. Join it at the bottom of the script

3 Drag the **if** block into your script, and drop it inside your **forever** block

4 Click the **Sensing** button above the Blocks Palette

5 Drag the **key space pressed?** block into your script and drop it into the frame of your **if** block. Click the menu in the block to select the **right arrow** key

Don't forget

You can refer back to the grid reference chart in Chapter 2 if you can't visualize how this movement is working.

68

Beware

Last chapter, you used the "when space key pressed" hat block. That's unsuitable for games that need fast fingers, because when you hold down a key, there's a delay before it repeats. Using the Sensing block as we have in this project enables the player to hold down the key to dash across the Stage.

6 Click the **Motion** button above the Blocks Palette. Drag the **change x by 10** block into the bracket of your **if** block. This block makes the sprite move right and will be run if the right arrow key is pressed

Hot tip

When you duplicate a block, it also duplicates the blocks joined inside or underneath it.

7 Right-click the **if** block and click **duplicate** in the menu. A copy of your **if** bracket and all its contents follows the mouse pointer. Click underneath your **if** bracket to add a copy of it there

8 Click the Sensing block in the copy to change the key to the **left arrow** key. Change the number in the **change x by 10** block to -10

9 Repeat this process to add controls for moving up and down. Instead of using the **change x by 10** block, use the **change y by 10** block. Remember, use 10 to go up, and use -10 to go down

Don't forget

To get rid of a block you no longer need in the Scripts Area, drag it into the Blocks Palette.

69

10 Test it by clicking the green flag and trying the cursor keys. You should see the cat move in four directions

Hot tip

Scratch won't let sprites walk off the edge of the Stage.

Adding more images

You've already learned how to add sprites to your project (see Chapter 3) and how to change the background (see Chapter 1), so use those skills to add the following:

1 Add the Beachball sprite. You can find it in the Things category in Scratch 2.0 (where it's called Beachball) and the Things folder in Scratch 1.4 (where it's called beachball1)

2 Add another cat sprite. It's in the Animals category in Scratch 2.0 and the Animals folder in Scratch 1.4. In Scratch 2.0, it's called Cat1. If you're using Scratch 1.4, you can choose to use either cat1-a or cat1-b

3 Add the background beach malibu in Scratch 2.0 or beach-malibu in Scratch 1.4. It's filed in the Nature Theme (Scratch 2.0) or folder (Scratch 1.4)

4 Your Stage should look something like this, although it doesn't matter where the sprites are positioned for now

Beware

Don't use the Bouncy Ball in Scratch 1.4 for this project. It looks the same but includes some scripts already, which we don't need.

Renaming sprites

As we add more sprites, it's important that we can easily understand which is which. In Scratch 1.4, sprites are just called Sprite1, Sprite2, and so on. Scratch 2.0 uses more descriptive names, but we now have sprites called Sprite1 and Cat1 which look identical. That could quickly get confusing. You can give sprites a name that makes it easier to write and understand your programs.

Rename your original cat sprite from Sprite1 to Cat, the ball to Beachball (only necessary in Scratch 1.4), and the second cat to Energy.

Renaming sprites in Scratch 2.0

1 Click the sprite in the Sprite List. A small information button appears in the corner of the sprite. Click it

2 Click in the box where it says Sprite1, delete that text and replace it with the new name

3 Click the **Back** button to the left of the sprite. It's a blue blob with a white triangle in it

Renaming sprites in Scratch 1.4

1 Click the sprite in the Sprite List to select it

2 Above the Scripts Area is a representation of the sprite, with its name beside it. Click in the name box, delete that text and type your new sprite name

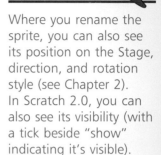

Hot tip

Where you rename the sprite, you can also see its position on the Stage, direction, and rotation style (see Chapter 2). In Scratch 2.0, you can also see its visibility (with a tick beside "show" indicating it's visible).

Don't forget

Short names are best: longer names are cut short in the Sprite List.

71

Beware

Make sure each sprite has a different name.

Making random numbers

One of the Operator blocks is used for making random numbers, and you can drag it into a number space in another block. Follow these steps to position the beachball in a random starting position, and facing a random direction:

1 Click the Beachball in the Sprite List, to make sure you're adding scripts to the right sprite. Click the **Scripts** tab to show the Scripts Area

2 Drag the **go to x:0 y:0** Motion block to the Scripts Area

3 Click the **Operators** button above the Blocks Palette. Drag the **pick random 1 to 10** block and drop it into the hole for the x coordinate. Do the same for the y coordinate

```
go to x: pick random 1 to 10  y: pick random 1 to 10
```

4 Click the numbers in the first **pick random** block and change them to -240 and 240

5 Click the numbers in the second **pick random** block and change them to -180 and 180

```
go to x: pick random -240 to 240  y: pick random -180 to 180
```

6 Use a similar process to make the ball point in a random direction too. Use the **point in direction** block, and pick a random number from -179 to 180

```
go to x: pick random -240 to 240  y: pick random -180 to 180
point in direction pick random -179 to 180
```

Moving the ball

The script to move the ball uses mostly blocks you've seen before, and just two new ones. Use your random positioning blocks as the starting point for the script to move the ball:

1 Add a **when green flag clicked** block above them

2 Click the **Looks** button above the Blocks Palette and drag in the **show** and **go to front** blocks. Join these underneath your random positioning blocks. The **go to front** block ensures that when the sprite hits the cat, the ball will be in front, so it looks more like a direct hit

```
when    clicked
go to x: pick random -240 to 240 y: pick random -180 to 180
point in direction pick random -179 to 180
show
go to front
```

3 Click the **Control** button above the Blocks Palette and drag in the **wait 1 secs** and **forever** blocks. Adjust the time delay to 3 seconds. The ball can appear anywhere, so the **wait** block gives the player time to move if the ball appears close to their starting position. The ball doesn't move or sap strength until after that grace period

4 Click the **Motion** button above the Blocks Palette and drag the **move 10 steps** and **if on edge, bounce** blocks into the **forever** block's bracket. The **if on edge, bounce** block changes the direction of the ball when it hits the edge of the Stage

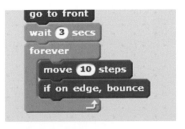

Hot tip

In Shop Cat (see Chapter 10), the "if on edge, bounce" block is used to make cars move left and right across the Stage.

73

...cont'd

5 Click the **Control** button above the Blocks Palette and drag in the **if** block

6 Click the **Sensing** button above the Blocks Palette and drag in the **touching?** block and set it to detect the Cat

7 Click the **Data** button (Scratch 2.0) or the **Variables** button (Scratch 1.4). Drag in the **change [variable name] by 1** block. Click the menu in the block to change the variable to the *strength*, and edit the value to -1

8 Click the green flag above the Stage and you should see the ball appear in a random location, and start moving in a random direction. You can move the cat, so why not see if you can dodge the ball?

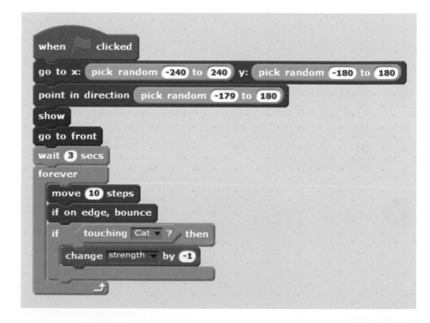

Right: the completed script.

Copying and deleting sprites

Now we've got one ball bouncing around, let's make it a bit more challenging! You can copy (or 'duplicate') your beachball sprite, including its scripts, so that when you play the game, you have several balls all bouncing around randomly. I recommend three:

1 Above the Stage is a toolbar containing four buttons. In Scratch 2.0, they're in the dark stripe at the top of the screen (right, top). In Scratch 1.4, they're in a rounded panel (above)

2 Click the first icon, which looks like a stamp. Your mouse pointer turns into a stamp

3 Click the Beachball on the Stage. A new sprite is added to your project, with the same scripts as the one you've duplicated

4 You can instead right-click on a sprite in the Sprite List to open a menu with the option to duplicate the sprite

5 You might want to delete a sprite, perhaps because you made too many duplicates, or because you want to tidy up sprites you created to try out the Paint Editor (see later in this Chapter). Click the scissors icon in the toolbar (see Step 1) and then click the sprite you want to delete

Hot tip

Use the two icons with four arrows on them to resize sprites (the one on the left enlarges, and the other one shrinks). Click one and then click the sprite on the Stage repeatedly to change its size. In Scratch 2.0, the tool stops when you move your pointer off the sprite. To stop using the tool in Scratch 1.4, click an empty part of the Stage, Sprite List or Scripts Area.

Beware

In most programs, a scissors icon is for cutting something you want to reuse later. In Scratch, it's for deleting sprites completely. If you delete one by mistake, open the Edit menu at the top of the screen and click Undelete.

Hot tip

Click the green flag and you should see several balls bouncing around.

...cont'd

Beware

Cloning is only available in Scratch 2.0. If you're using Scratch 1.4, you can't try this.

Cloning sprites (Scratch 2.0)

Scratch 2.0 introduced a new feature: the ability to clone sprites. This means that a sprite can make a copy of itself or another sprite while the game is running. This is a more elegant solution than duplicating sprites yourself, for four reasons:

- The program does the donkey work of making the copies, so it saves you time.

- The clones can be made at any time while the game is running, so you can respond to what the player does. You could have monsters or treasure multiplying, for example, depending on what the player does.

- There's just one set of scripts to edit when you want to make changes. With duplicated sprites, you would have to make changes to the scripts on all of them, if you wanted to change the speed of the balls, for example. With cloned sprites, there's just one sprite to change and the copies of that are made during the game.

- It's easier to understand how the program works, because there are no identical scripts in the program while you're editing it.

Don't forget

Duplicating sprites is when you make a copy of a sprite while you're writing the game. Cloning is when Scratch makes a copy of a sprite while the game is running.

There are three main blocks that are used for managing clones:

- **create clone of myself**: This block creates a copy of the sprite. It also enables you to create a copy of another sprite by clicking the menu in the block and choosing another sprite.

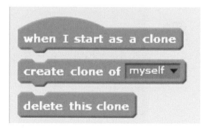

- **when I start as a clone**: This hat block is used at the top of a script you would like to run when the clone is created.

- **delete this clone**: This block is used to delete a clone. No other block can be joined underneath it.

Hot tip

For another example of cloning sprites in Scratch 2.0, see Going Batty in Chapter 9.

Let's look on the next page at how we can use cloning to make the game start easy and get gradually harder, as new balls appear during gameplay.

...cont'd

1 First, delete any duplicates you made of the Beachball sprite. Click the scissors icon in the dark stripe at the top of the screen, and then click the duplicate sprite on the Stage or in the Sprite List. Repeat until there's just one beachball left

2 Click the Beachball in the Sprite List. In the Scripts Area, remove the **when green flag clicked** hat block from your script. Click the second block in the stack (the **go to** block), and drag it away from the hat block. Keep the **when green flag clicked** block in the Scripts Area

3 Click the **Control** button above the Blocks Palette. Drag in the **when I start as a clone** hat block, and join this to the top of your script

Hot tip

when I start as a clone

go to x: pick random -240 to 240 y: pick random -180 to 180

point in direction pick random -179 to 180

show

You can change the wait time to adjust how long there is before each ball appears, and you can increase the number of balls by changing the number of times the loop that creates them repeats. Cloning makes it simple to make changes like this, which would be quite fiddly if you were using duplicated sprites instead.

4 Add the following blocks to the **when green flag clicked** block. You can find the **hide** block by clicking the **Looks** button above the Blocks Palette. The rest are Control blocks

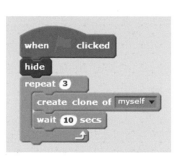

The **hide** block is there because the original beachball is only used to make copies of itself. It's the clones that do the bouncing. When the green flag is clicked, the beachball makes three clones of itself, ten seconds apart. When each clone is created, it uses the same script you used previously to move to a random position, pause briefly and then start bouncing around.

Adding the energy meter

We're going to show the player how much energy they have left using an energy meter, which is a picture of the player's character (the cat), that changes its size as the player loses or gains energy:

Above: the energy meter's ghost effect means the background shines through.

1 Click the Energy sprite in the Sprite List to select it

2 Above the Blocks Palette, click the **Events** button in Scratch 2.0, or the **Control** button in Scratch 1.4. Drag the **when green flag clicked** block into the Scripts Area

3 In Scratch 2.0, click the **Data** button above the Blocks Palette. In Scratch 1.4, click the **Variables** button

4 Drag in the **set score to 0** block and join it to the **when green flag clicked** block. Change the variable in the block to *strength*, and the number to 100. This ensures the strength is set to its maximum value as the game starts

5 Click the **Motion** button above the Blocks Palette and drag in the **go to x:0 y:0** block. Change the numbers in it to x:-190 and y:120. This puts the energy meter in the top left corner of the screen

6 Click the **Looks** button above the Blocks Palette and drag in the **set color effect to 0** block. Change the effect to ghost, and the number to 50. This makes our energy meter semi-transparent, so it doesn't look like a character in the game (see Figure 1, facing page)

7 Click the **Control** button above the Blocks Palette. Drag in the **forever** block, and add an **if** block inside its bracket (see Figure 2, facing page)

8 The **if** block is used to check whether the player has run out of strength, which will be when the *strength* variable is less than 1. Click the **Operators** button above the Blocks Palette and drag the < block into the **if** block (see Figure 3). This checks whether the number on the left is less than the number on the right

9 Click the **Data** or **Variables** button above the Blocks Palette. Drag the *strength* variable block into the left of the Operator block. Type a 1 into the right of that block. This will check whether the strength is less than 1, and will do whatever is inside the **if** bracket if it is

10 Click the **Looks** button above the Blocks Palette and drag the **say Hello! for 2 secs** block into the **if** bracket. Change the text in it to Game Over

11 Click the **Control** button above the Blocks Palette and drag the **stop all** block into the **if** bracket. This will stop the game if the *strength* variable is less than 1

12 Finally, you need to make the energy meter change its size. Click the **Looks** button above the Blocks Palette and drag in the **set size to 100%** block. It goes inside the **forever** bracket, but outside the **if** bracket. Click **Data** or **Variables** above the Blocks Palette, and drag the *strength* variable block into its number space (see Figure 4, right)

Figure 1.

Figure 2.

Figure 3.

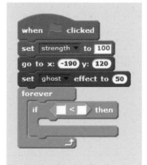

Figure 4.

Beware

If you just check whether *strength* is equal to zero, the game might never end. A ball could be sapping the player's energy, and could take the *strength* variable into negative numbers before the program checked whether the strength was zero and stopped the game.

Hot tip

If you're using a Raspberry Pi and you hid the score on the Stage to speed the game up, click the Variables button above the Blocks Palette and drag the "show variable score" block into your script, immediately above the "stop all" block.

Painting in Scratch

Scratch includes a Paint Editor you can use to design your own sprites and backgrounds, or to edit the existing ones. There isn't an ice cream sprite provided with Scratch, so you'll need to use the Paint Editor to make one for the Super Dodgeball game.

The layout of the tools is different in Scratch 2.0 and Scratch 1.4.

Painting in Scratch 2.0

To create a new sprite, click the **Paint new sprite** button above the Sprite List. It's the second of the four buttons.

The Paint Editor opens on the right of the screen. You can increase the amount of space available for drawing by shrinking the size of the Stage. To do that, click **Edit** at the top of the screen and then click **Small stage layout**. When you've finished painting, repeat the process to return the Stage to its normal size.

The chequered area is the canvas, and the painting tools are arranged around the sides of it. Refer to the picture below as you learn about the tools on the following pages.

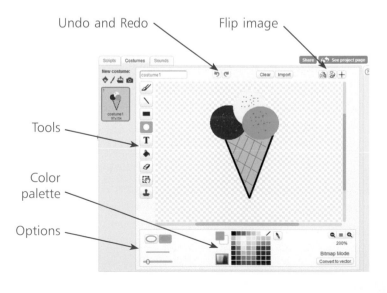

Hot tip

You can use the Paint Editor to customize the sprites that come with Scratch too. Click your sprite in the Sprite List to select it, then click the Costumes tab above the Blocks Palette. In Scratch 2.0, that takes you straight into the Paint Editor. In Scratch 1.4, you open the Paint Editor by clicking the Edit button beside the costume you want to redesign.

Beware

In Scratch 2.0, your changes are saved automatically. If you want to play around with the Paint Editor, start a new sprite, rather than editing one you will need later.

80

Painting in Scratch 1.4

In Scratch 1.4, you create a new sprite by clicking the **Paint new sprite** button above the Sprite List. It's the first of the three buttons.

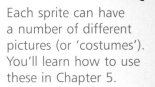
The Paint Editor opens in a new window, with the controls down the left and the canvas you paint on on the right.

Refer to the picture below to orientate yourself as you read about the tools available on the following pages.

Grow and Shrink   Rotate   Flip image   Undo and Redo

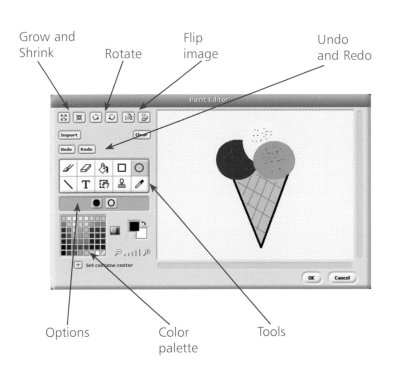

Options   Color palette   Tools

Using Paint tools

To select one of the tools, just click its icon in the Paint Editor. I've shown icons for both versions of Scratch, where they differ:

- **Paintbrush**: Simply hold down the mouse button as you move your pointer over the canvas, and you leave a line behind you. In the options, use the slider in Scratch 2.0 or the menu in Scratch 1.4 to change the thickness of the brush.

- **Line**: Click at the start of the line, hold the mouse button down, and then move the mouse to the end of the line. When you release the mouse button, a straight line is drawn between where you clicked and where you released the mouse button.

- **Rectangle**: Click to position one corner, hold the mouse button down, and then drag to the opposite corner and release the button. In the options, you can choose whether the shape is filled or hollow. Immediately after drawing the shape, you can use the handles on it to resize it in Scratch 2.0.

- **Ellipse**: This works in a similar way to the rectangle tool. Click, hold down the mouse button and drag the mouse pointer to create an ellipse. The ellipse expands to fill the space between where you click and where you release the mouse button.

- **Text** in Scratch 2.0: Click where you would like to place text on the canvas and then type what you'd like to write. Press Enter to start a new line. Press the mouse button when you've finished and a box appears around the text.

You can reposition the text by clicking and dragging inside the box, resize it by dragging one of the drag points on its sides and corners, and can rotate it by dragging the small circle above it. When you click outside the box, the editing ends. In Scratch 2.0, you can have multiple text boxes on a sprite, but you can't reposition them or edit them later (unless you're working in vector mode, coming right up!).

- **Text** in Scratch 1.4: To reposition your text, click and drag the box that appears in its top left corner. You can edit and move the text again later by selecting the Text tool again, but you can only have one piece of text per sprite. Use Enter to start a new line when you're typing your text. In the options area, you can change the font and text size.

Above: Fades are available in the fill options.

- **Fill**: This will fill a shape on your image with color. In the options area, you can choose a different pattern to use, with the foreground color fading into the background (see right).

- **Eraser**: This works like the Paintbrush, except that it deletes your image. Click once to delete just one spot, or click and drag to remove larger parts of the image. You can change the size of the eraser in the options area.

- **Select**: If you want to modify, move or delete a part of your image, use this tool to select it first. It can only select areas that are rectangular. Click in one corner of the area you'd like to select, drag the mouse pointer to the opposite corner, and release the mouse button. You can then click inside the selected area and drag it to move it, press the Delete key on the keyboard to remove it, and flip it upside down or reverse it horizontally. In Scratch 1.4, you can also rotate it, enlarge it or shrink it.

- **Stamp**: The stamp tool enables you to copy part of your image and then paste it somewhere else in it. You could use it to make a sprite's two eyes identical, for example. After selecting the tool, click and drag a rectangular box on the image to select part of it. In Scratch 2.0, click in the middle of the box and drag the copy to position it. Click outside it to drop it in place. In Scratch 1.4, move the mouse pointer and click to stamp the image in place. You can stamp the same image fragment multiple times (in Scratch 1.4 only).

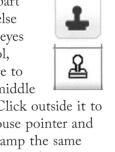

Beware

In Scratch 2.0, you can only use the Stamp tool to paste one copy and then you have to start over, selecting the area you want to copy. After you've used it, the Select tool is chosen, so remember to choose the Stamp tool again if you want to use it again straight away.

Using colors

There is a palette of 56 colors you can click to choose a color for the art tools in the Paint Editor. The palettes are organized slightly differently in Scratch 2.0 (left, below) and Scratch 1.4 (right, below).

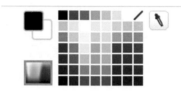
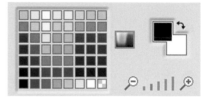

The palette includes a transparent color, which enables you to erase parts of your drawing so the background shines through. In Scratch 2.0, it's represented by a red diagonal line through a white box, and is in the top right of the palette. In Scratch 1.4, it's the chequered box in the palette, the last box in the bottom row.

When you click the rainbow colored box beside the palette, the palette offers a much richer range of colors for you to pick from.

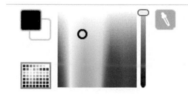

The two overlapping boxes beside the palette are used to switch between choosing the foreground and background colors. These are used to choose the two colors in a fading pattern fill. Click the overlapping boxes to alternate between the foreground and background and then choose your color. Unless you're using a fading fill, you probably won't need to use this feature.

The pipette tool is on the right of the palette in Scratch 2.0, and on the toolbar in Scratch 1.4 (see icon on the right). When you click it, you can choose a color by clicking it on the canvas. This is the perfect tool if you need to precisely match a color you've already used in your drawing.

Using vectors in Scratch 2.0

Scratch 2.0 introduced support for vector images, which look better when they're resized, but are much more difficult to draw. Here's how to create them.

- Click the **Convert to Vector Mode** button at the bottom of the Paint Editor. The vector drawing tools are on the right.

- Click the pencil tool to draw on the canvas. Press the mouse button and drag the mouse pointer to make a line.

- The line, rectangle and ellipse tools enable you to draw in the same way as you do in the bitmap mode.

- You can fill rectangles and ellipses. To draw a shape with the pencil that you can fill, you need to join up your line's start and finishing points. You can fill the pencil line itself too.

- The select tool (with an arrow icon) enables you to edit shapes you added to the canvas previously. Click a shape and you can drag it to reposition it, or click and drag the handles on its sides and corners to resize it.

- With the reshape tool (see right), you can click the round control points that appear on a line (see below) and drag them to reshape the line.

- To copy a shape, click the stamp tool in the toolbar and then click the shape you'd like to copy.

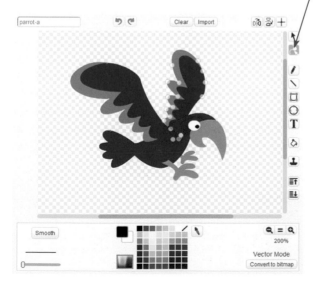

Hot tip

Bitmap images store all the dots that make up the picture, and this image type is used in Scratch 1.4 and Scratch 2.0. A vector image stores instructions, explaining where the lines are and how to draw the image. Only Scratch 2.0 supports vector images.

Don't forget

Instead of using the paint tools to color in dots on the canvas to build up your picture, as you did in the Paint Editor previously, the vector tools create lines and shapes which you can edit later.

Beware

If you convert a vector image to a bitmap, the outlines become fuzzy and you'll lose the ability to edit the vector shapes. Don't do it, unless you're sure you know what you're doing!

Making the ice cream appear

After all that hard work, you deserve an ice cream! You need to add two scripts to the ice cream sprite: this first one makes it appear in random locations for a short while and then disappear:

1 Drag in the **when green flag clicked** block. I'm sure you know where to find it by now! It's an Events block in Scratch 2.0, and a Control block in Scratch 1.4

2 Click the **Looks** button above the Blocks Palette. Drag in the **go to front** and **go back 1 layers** blocks. This means the ice cream will appear behind the beachballs, which looks most natural

3 It's easier to draw sprites large, so my ice cream sprite was huge. I used the **set size** block to reduce its size to 30%. You can use a similar block, and adjust the size to what you need

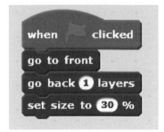

4 Click the **Control** button above the Blocks Palette and drag the **forever** block in to your script

5 Click the **Motion** button above the Blocks Palette and add the **go to x:0 y:0** block

6 Click the **Operators** button above the Blocks Palette and add two **pick random 1 to 10** Operator blocks in the number spaces in the **go to** block. Edit the numbers as you did for the beachball to position the ice cream in a random position on the Stage, where x is a random number between -240 and 240, and y is a random number between -180 and 180

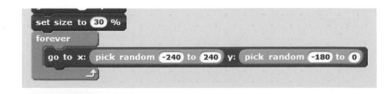

7 Click the **Looks** button above the Blocks Palette and drag the **show** and **hide** blocks into your script

```
when       clicked
go to front
go back ❶ layers
set size to ❸❶ %
forever
    go to x:  pick random -240 to 240  y:  pick random -180 to 0
    show
    hide
```

8 Click the **Control** button above the Blocks Palette and drag two **wait 1 secs** blocks into your script, after each of the **show** and **hide** blocks

9 Click the **Operators** button above the Blocks Palette and drag a **pick random 1 to 10** block into each of the wait blocks. Adjust the numbers in the **pick random** blocks, so the ice cream is shown for between 5 and 10 seconds, and hidden for between 1 and 3 seconds

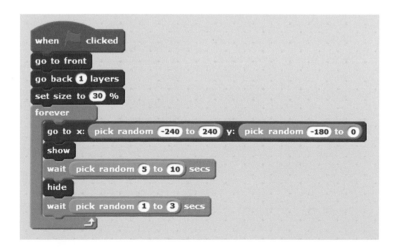

Hot tip

The ice cream in Super Dodgeball not only provides a scoring mechanism and a way to replenish strength. It also forces players to move around the screen, so they can't just find a safe place and stay there!

Enabling the player to score

The other script you need to add to your ice cream detects when the player reaches it, and then increases the score and strength:

1 Drag in the **when green flag clicked** block

2 Click the **Control** button above the Blocks Palette and drag the **forever** block in to your script

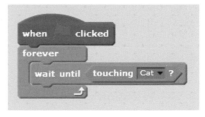

3 Add the **wait until** block into your script. It's another Control block

4 Click the **Sensing** button above the Blocks Palette. Drag the **touching?** block into the space in your **wait until** block, and then click the menu in

it to choose the Cat. This block will pause this script until the cat is touching the ice cream

5 If the cat's touching the ice cream, we need to increase the *score* and the *strength* variables! Click the **Data** or **Variables** button above the Blocks Palette. Drag in two copies of the **change score by 1** block. Click the menu in one of the blocks to choose the *strength* variable, and change the number to 10 in both blocks

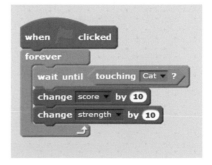

Don't forget

A sprite can have more than one script triggered by the green flag. We're using two on the ice cream.

6 At the moment, it's possible for the player's strength to be more than 100, if they collect an ice cream before being hit by a ball, for example. We need to make sure the strength doesn't go above 100. Click the **Control** button above the Blocks Palette and drag in the **if** block

7 Click the **Operators** button above the Blocks Palette, and drag the > block into the space in the **if** block

8 Click the **Data** or **Variables** button above the Blocks Palette. Drag the *strength* variable into the left of the > block, and type 100 in the right of it

9 Drag the **set score to 0** block into the bracket of the **if** block. Change the variable in it to *strength*, and the value in it to 100. That will ensure that if the *strength* variable is even higher than 100, it is instead set to be exactly 100

10 Finally, click the **Looks** button above the Blocks Palette and drag the **hide** block into the end of your **forever** loop. This will hide the ice cream if the cat touches it, making it look like the cat has picked it up

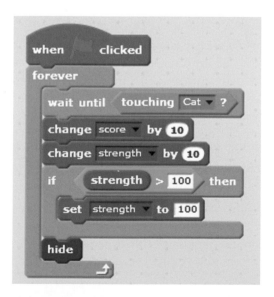

Hot tip

Some of these ideas can be used in other Scratch games you make too.

Hot tip

You could stop the ice cream from replenishing the player's strength, if the game's too easy.

Hot tip

Don't be afraid to experiment and see what happens if you change numbers around, or add in your own effects. Click File and choose Save as a copy (in Scratch 2.0) or Save As (in Scratch 1.4), and your project will be saved with a new name, leaving the previous version untouched. If your game stops working, you can always go back to the previous version you made.

Tweaking the gameplay

If you find the game is too easy or too difficult, there are several things you can do to adjust the speed and difficulty of the game:

- To slow down the ball, change the number in its **move 10 steps** block to a lower number.

- To speed up the ball, change the number in its **move 10 steps** block to a higher number.

- To give players more time to react when a ball appears near them, change the number in the **wait 3 secs** block to a higher number.

- To make it easier to dodge the balls, make them smaller. You can do this by adding a **set size to 100%** block under the **when green flag clicked** block in their scripts. Change the number from 100% to something smaller. Remember that if you're using duplicated ball sprites (rather than cloned sprites in Scratch 2.0), you'll need to make this change for each one.

- To make it easier to catch the ice cream, make it bigger. Change the number in its **set size to 30% block** to a greater number.

- To give players more time to catch the ice cream, you can adjust the random numbers used to decide how long it's on screen. After its **show** block, change the random waiting time to a minimum of 10 seconds and a maximum of 20 seconds, to give players twice as long.

- To make the energy last twice as long, change how much energy the ball saps when it touches the cat from 1 to 0.5. Click the ball sprite and edit the **change strength by -1** block to **change strength by -0.5**. If you're using duplicated ball sprites, you'll need to change each ball sprite's script.

When you design games, you'll often find you need to adjust things like this to make the difficulty just right: a bit challenging, but not so difficult that it's not fun to play.

Professional game designers get other people to test their games, and watch them to see how easy or difficult they find them. Lots of people who use Scratch put their games on the Scratch website for others to try and give them feedback on too (see Chapter 11).

5 Cosmic Chorus

In this chapter, you get to conduct an alien choir, triggering samples and musical notes with your computer keyboard. You'll learn how to add sound effects and musical notes to your projects, how to animate sprites with multiple pictures, how to communicate between sprites, and how to add a title screen to your programs. You'll also learn how you can use Scratch to compose music or play your favorite tunes.

Introducing Cosmic Chorus

In Cosmic Chorus, you conduct an alien choir by pressing keys on the keyboard. You use the top row of letter keys to control which notes the soloist sings, and press the keys 1 to 5 to tell the backing singers to make their sounds.

You can have fun playing around with the project as an instrument, and you can customize it with your own sounds.

This project teaches you some important Scratch techniques:

- Two different ways of making sounds in Scratch, by playing short recordings, and by asking the computer to play a particular note using a simulated instrument.

- How to add a title screen to a project.

- How to get one sprite to control another sprite.

- How to animate a sprite using multiple costumes.

Now that you've completed several Scratch projects, you're an expert on the basics. In this chapter, I'll assume that you know how to add blocks to a script, and where to find the blocks you've used often before, such as the **when green flag clicked** block, and the **go to x:0 y:0** block.

Beware

At the time of writing, many of the audio samples and the different simulated instruments aren't working in the Raspberry Pi version of Scratch. You can still make music and play other recorded sounds.

Adding sprites and costumes

Each sprite can have more than one picture, or "costume", as they are known in Scratch. That enables you to change the appearance of a sprite while your program is running, so you can give it facial expressions or body movements, for example. In this project, you're going to use the Gobo sprite, a friendly-looking spiky alien.

Adding costumes in Scratch 2.0

1 Above the Sprite List, click the first New sprite button to add a sprite from the library

2 Click the Fantasy category and click Gobo. You're told the sprite has three costumes. Click the **OK** button at the bottom of the window to bring Gobo into your project

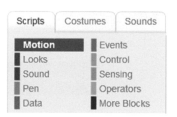

3 Above the Blocks Palette, click the **Costumes** tab

4 The Costumes Area shows you the three costumes for Gobo. Underneath each one is its name (e.g. gobo-a) and size (93 units wide by 109 high). On the right is the Paint Editor (the chequered area), so you can redesign the costume. Above the Paint Editor is a box where you can rename the costume (here, gobo-a)

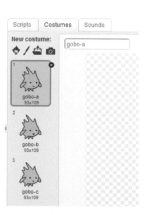

Hot tip

To delete a costume in Scratch 2.0, click it in the Costumes Area, and then click the X in the top-right corner of the costume. You aren't prompted to confirm, but you can go to the Edit menu and click Undelete if you make a mistake.

Beware

In Scratch 2.0, a sprite can include several costumes. In Scratch 1.4, you have to add each costume separately.

...cont'd

5 If you wanted to add another costume to this sprite, you could click one of the new costume buttons at the top of the Costumes Area. You can add a costume from the library, paint one, upload a picture from your computer or use your webcam to take a picture

6 To make a copy of a costume, you right-click it and then choose to duplicate it

7 To get back to the Scripts Area, click the **Scripts** tab above the Costumes Area

Adding costumes in Scratch 1.4

In Scratch 1.4, you have to add each costume to the Gobo sprite individually.

1 Above the Sprite List, click the middle New sprite button to add a sprite from the library

Hot tip

In both Scratch 2.0 and Scratch 1.4, you can manage the costumes for any sprite at any time. Click it in the Sprite List first, and then click the Costumes tab.

2 Go into the Fantasy folder. There are three sprites called gobo1, gobo2, and gobo3. These are the same character with different expressions, and we'll use them as different costumes on a single sprite. Add gobo1

...cont'd

3 Above the Scripts Area, click the **Costumes** tab. You can see the costume you've added already, together with buttons to edit it, copy it (which makes a new costume that looks the same), and an **X** button to delete it. You can edit its name (gobo1) in the text box

Hot tip

Copying costumes is useful for animation. Using the Paint Editor, you can make small changes to the copied costume, so that when you switch between the costumes, the sprite appears to move.

4 At the top of the Costumes Area are three buttons to add a new costume by painting one, importing one or using your webcam. Click the **Import** button

5 The Sprite Library opens again, as it did in Step 2. This time, choose gobo2

6 Repeat Steps 4 and 5 to add the gobo3 costume too

7 To get back to the Scripts Area, click the **Scripts** tab above the Costumes Area

Preparing Cosmic Chorus

Before you start to make the Cosmic Chorus project, prepare the other graphics you'll need:

1 You should already have the Gobo sprite with three costumes on it in your project

2 You should also still have the cat sprite: we'll use the cat to conduct the chorus, even though it won't be shown on the Stage

3 Change the background of the Stage to the moon picture. It is in the Space theme in Scratch 2.0 and the Nature folder in Scratch 1.4

4 You need to add another sprite from the library to use as your soloist. If you're using Scratch 2.0, add the Pico sprite. It includes four wonderful expressions

Above: Your starting graphics for Cosmic Chorus in Scratch 2.0 (top, with Pico) and in Scratch 1.4 (bottom, with the fantasy-1a costume showing).

5 If you're using Scratch 1.4, click the button to add a new sprite from the library, and then add fantasy1-b as your soloist. Follow the steps you used when adding the Gobo costumes earlier, to give this new sprite another costume too: fantasy1-a. I've suggested adding them in this order so that the first costume is the "quiet" one, and the second costume is the "singing" one. The first costume is used until you change it

Adding sounds to a sprite

There are two different ways you can add sounds and music to your scripts in Scratch:

- You can play a recording of a sound effect or a piece of music. Scratch has a library of sound effects you can use, or you can add your own sounds.

- You can tell the computer to play particular notes or drumbeats to create a piece of music.

We'll use our Gobo sprite to play a sound recording, and our soloist to "sing" musical notes. First, let's add the sound to Gobo.

Adding sounds in Scratch 2.0

1 Click the Gobo sprite in the Sprite List, and click the **Sounds** tab. It's beside the **Scripts** and **Costumes** tabs

2 The Sounds Area looks a bit like the Costumes Area: down the left there is a list of the sounds the sprite has. The Gobo sprite starts with a pop sound. You can click the **Play** button on the right to hear it. The big space on the right shows you the waveform, which is a picture of the sound: the shape is taller when the sound is louder

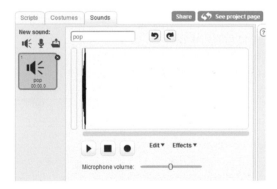

3 At the top of the Sounds Area are three New sound buttons to add a sound from the library, record a sound using your microphone, or upload a sound recording from your computer. Click the small speaker icon to choose a sound from the library

97

Hot tip

If you have a webcam, it probably has a microphone built in to it, so you can use that for recording your own sounds.

Hot tip

If you can't decide which sound to add, I recommend using one of the beat box or singer sounds in the Vocals category or folder for this project.

Beware

In Scratch 2.0, don't confuse the tiny new sound button with the large picture of a speaker used to represent a sound effect on a sprite. They use the same image, confusingly!

...cont'd

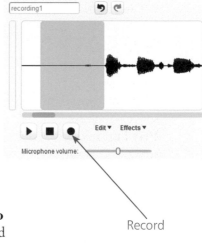

Above: You are likely to see a warning from the Flash player and might be warned by your browser too. These alerts make sure your camera and microphone are only used with your permission. If you see a warning when you are trying to use the camera or microphone, click Allow.

4 The Sound Library is similar to the Sprite Library. You can choose a category on the left, and use the scrollbar on the right to find more sounds. To preview a sound click the **Play** button beside its speaker icon

5 Add a sound you like by double-clicking it

Recording sounds in Scratch 2.0

If you prefer, you can record your own sound using a microphone connected to your computer, or your webcam:

1 Click the **Microphone** button at the top of the Sounds Area. A new empty sound is added to your sprite

2 Click the round **Record** button (see picture) and talk, sing or shout at your microphone!

3 If you need to trim silence off the start or end of your sound, click and drag in the waveform to select part of it. The selected part is tinted blue. Click the **Edit** menu underneath, and then choose **Delete** to remove the silence. If you make a mistake, click the **Undo** button (an arrow curved to the left) above the waveform

Record

Sounds in Scratch 1.4

The way sounds are managed is different in Scratch 1.4, so follow these instructions to give Gobo a voice:

1   Click the Gobo sprite in the Sprite List, and then click the **Sounds** tab, next to the **Scripts** and **Costumes** tabs

2   You can either record a sound or import one from the Sound Library. Click the **Import** button

3   The Sound Library is similar to the Sprite Library. There are several folders of sounds to browse

4   Click a sound once to hear it. To add it to your sprite, click it and then click the **OK** button. Find a sound you like and add it

5   In the Sounds Area, you can see the sound you've added to your sprite. Click the **Play** button or the speaker icon to hear it. Click the **X** button to delete it. You can also rename the sound in the text box

Hot tip

The number underneath the sound name shows you its duration in hours:minutes:seconds format.

Recording in Scratch 1.4

You can also record your own sounds in Scratch 1.4 using a microphone, so Gobo can sing with your own voice:

1 If you prefer to record your own sound, click the **Record** button at the top of the Sounds Area

2 The Sound Recorder opens. To start recording, click the **Record** button with a red circle on it. The green bars indicate the volume, stretching to the right as the sound gets louder. When you've finished recording, click the **Stop** button with a square on it

3 Listen to your sound by clicking the **Play** button with a green triangle on it

4 If you're happy with the sound, click **OK** to add it to your sprite. If not, you can record another sound or click **Cancel** to close the Sound Recorder without adding a sound to your sprite

5 Your sound is added with the name recording1. You can click this and edit it in the Sounds Area if you'd like to give it a more memorable name. Each sprite can have several sounds, so it helps if they have names that enable you to tell them apart

Playing sounds

You can find the blocks used for playing your sound effects by clicking the **Sound** button above the Blocks Palette, as shown below on the left in Scratch 2.0 and on the right in Scratch 1.4.

Beware

Some of the sounds supplied with Scratch 1.4 don't work on the Raspberry Pi.

The blocks are:

- **play sound [soundname]**: Use this block to play a sound you've added to the current sprite. Choose a different sound by clicking the menu in this block. There's a shortcut in this menu you can use to record a new sound.

- **play sound [soundname] until done**: This block plays your sound, but waits until it's finished playing before the next block in your stack is run.

- **stop all sounds**: This block silences Scratch. It stops the sound recordings, and also stops the notes and drums.

- **change volume by -10**: This block turns the volume down by 10%. You can change the number in the block, and make it a positive number to increase the volume. The volume affects both the sound effects and the notes and drums.

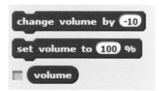

- **set volume to 100%**: Change the number in this block to set to volume to your chosen level.

- **volume**: This is a variable that contains the current volume level, from 0 to 100.

Don't forget

Before a sprite can play a sound from the library or a sound recording, you must add the sound to that sprite. If you've added a sound and don't see it in the "play sound" block's menu, make sure you've selected the right sprite in the Sprite List.

Hot tip

You can add more than one sound to each sprite.

Making Gobo sing

Let's make the scripts to make Gobo sing! We're going to add two separate scripts to Gobo:

1 Click Gobo in the Sprite List to make sure you're adding scripts to the right sprite, and click the **Scripts** tab if necessary to open the Scripts Area

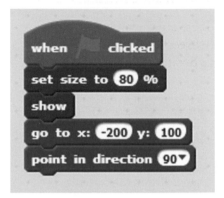

2 To get your Gobo ready to sing, add the first script that positions it in the right place

3 You also need to add a stack of blocks that will make it sing. Add the following blocks, but don't join them to your other script. If you're using Scratch 1.4, the costume names you need are gobo3 (in place of gobo-c) and gobo1 (in place of gobo-a)

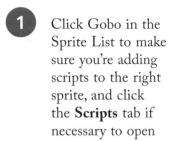

4 Click this script to see the Gobo jump up slightly (by changing the y coordinate), open its mouth (by changing the costume to an open-mouthed picture), sing the sound effect, then close its mouth (by changing the costume back) and land again

Using broadcasts

You can't make one sprite move or control another sprite, but you can get sprites to cooperate by exchanging messages with each other. That's a much more polite way to do things!

There are three blocks that are used for managing broadcasts between sprites. In Scratch 2.0, they are brown Events blocks, but in Scratch 1.4, they are yellow Control blocks.

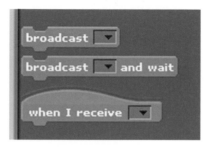

Here's how you use the blocks:

- **broadcast [message]**: This block sends a message out from one sprite to all the other sprites and the background, although you probably won't want them all to respond to that message. You can choose the content of the message, which is just a short piece of text. Click the menu in the block and you can set up a new message, or choose one of the messages you set up previously.

- **when I receive [message]**: This hat block is used to start a script when a certain message is broadcast from any sprite. You can choose which message, or create a new message, from the menu in the block.

- **broadcast [message] and wait**: This block broadcasts a message, but it then waits until any scripts that the message starts have finished. Imagine you used this block to broadcast a message that told a sprite to move. This block would wait until after that sprite had finished moving.

To make it easy to understand your program, set up messages that describe what you're coordinating. It's more meaningful to have a message called "move ship", for example, than "message1".

Hot tip

You can also use messages to coordinate between different scripts on the same sprite (see Chapter 7).

Conducting the Gobo

Follow these steps to make the cat tell the Gobo when to sing:

1 Click the cat sprite in the Sprite List

2 Add the following script to the cat. To add the key sensing block, drag in the **key space pressed?** block, and use the menu in it to change the key to 1

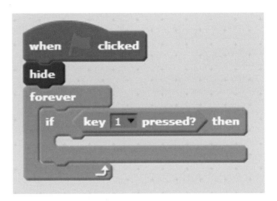

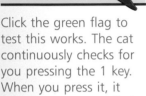

Hot tip

Click the green flag to test this works. The cat continuously checks for you pressing the 1 key. When you press it, it sends a message called sing-1. When the Gobo receives that message, it jumps for joy and sings!

3 Drag in the **broadcast [message] and wait** block and put it inside your **if** bracket

4 Click the menu in your **broadcast [message] and wait** block. Click **new message** (in Scratch 2.0) or **new** (in Scratch 1.4)

5 Enter the message sing-1 and click **OK**

Don't forget

The broadcast blocks are Events blocks in Scratch 2.0, and Control blocks in Scratch 1.4.

6 Click the Gobo in the Sprite List. Drag the **when I receive sing-1** block into the Scripts Area and join it to the top of the script that makes Gobo sing

Adding more Gobos

To make it a choir, let's add some more Gobos!

1 Right-click on Gobo in the Sprite List and when the menu opens click **duplicate**. Repeat this three more times, so you have a total of five Gobos

Beware

Don't forget to click the Gobo you want in the Sprite List before adding new sounds or editing scripts.

105

2 Click each duplicate Gobo in the Sprite List and edit their **go to x:-200 y:100** blocks in the green flag script. For two of them, edit the **point in direction 90** block too, so all the Gobos face the middle. Use these values:

- x:0 y:100

- x:200 y:100; point in direction -90

- x:-100 y:50

- x:100 y:50; point in direction -90

3 For the two Gobos that face left, fix their rotation styles to left-right (see Chapter 2)

4 Click each Gobo in the Sprite List, add a different sound to it, and change its **play sound [soundname] until done** block to play that sound

5 We want the Gobos to sing independently. Click each one in the Sprite List in turn, and click the menu in the **when I receive sing-1** hat block to create a new message. For your duplicate Gobos, use the messages sing-2, sing-3, sing-4 and sing-5. Each Gobo should be looking for a different message

Hot tip

When typing into the "go to x:0 y:0" block in Scratch 1.4, you can press the Tab key on your keyboard to move between the x and y spaces in the block.

...cont'd

If you click "delete"
instead of "duplicate"
in the menu by mistake,
click Edit at the top of
the screen and then
choose Undelete.

Putting all the keyboard
detection on one sprite
like this makes it easier
to understand and edit
the program and its
controls.

6 Click the cat sprite in the Sprite List. In its script, right-click on the **if** block and choose **duplicate**. When you duplicate a block, it also copies the blocks that are underneath or inside it. In this case, duplicating the **if** block also copies the Sensing block for the keypress that is in the **if** block's frame, and the **broadcast [message] and wait** block that is inside its bracket. Click at the bottom of your **if** block to paste the copy there. Now you have two **if** blocks with their associated Sensing and broadcast blocks. Click on the top **if** block and duplicate it, and this time you'll add two copies of it, because the one you just added underneath is duplicated too. Click the bottom **if** block and duplicate it to add your fifth and final set of blocks for sensing keypresses and broadcasting the messages that make the Gobos sing

7 Edit your duplicated scripts to change the keys detected to 2, 3, 4, and 5, and the messages sent to sing-2, sing-3, sing-4 and sing-5

8 Click the green flag button above the Stage to test your program works. When you press the keys 1 to 5, it should trigger a different Gobo to jump and sing

Playing music in Scratch

As well as playing sound recordings, you can program Scratch to generate music using drums and simulated instruments. The blocks to do this are all in the Sound section of the Blocks Palette. Whether you know how to make music already or not, you can use Scratch to write your own tunes with these blocks:

Don't forget

See Playing Sounds, earlier in this chapter, for a guide to the volume blocks.

- **play drum 1 for 0.2 beats**: You can click the number 1 to open a menu and choose a different type of drum. This block only plays the drum once, but you can change how many beats (or how much time) that drum takes up.

- **rest for 0.2 beats**: Use this block to add a short silence (a rest) in your music.

- **play note 60 for 0.5 beats**: The number 60 is for the note known as middle C. Higher numbers are higher notes, and lower numbers are lower notes. Click the 60 to open a menu that helps you choose the note by its name. In Scratch 1.4, this includes a piano picture (see below).

- **set instrument to 1**: Click the 1 to choose from over 20 simulated instruments. Instrument 1 is the piano.

- **set tempo to 60 bpm**: This sets the tempo (or speed) of your music at 60 beats per minute.

- **change tempo by 20**: Use this block to make your music faster, or use a negative number to slow it down.

- **tempo**: You can use this variable to find out what the current tempo (speed) of the music is.

Beware

At the time of writing, there's a bug in Scratch on the Raspberry Pi which makes all the instruments sound the same.

play note 60 for 0.5 beats

C (60)

Adding the singing soloist

You can use these blocks to make the soloist sing different notes depending on which keys you press:

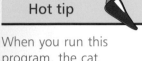
1 Create a variable called *note*, and make it for all sprites. Untick its box in the Blocks Palette so it isn't shown on the Stage

2 Click your soloist sprite in the Sprite List and create this script in its Scripts Area

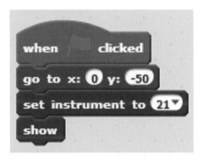

3 Drag in the **when I receive [message]** hat block and click the menu in it to create a new message. I've called it pico-sing, because my soloist is called Pico and this message tells it to sing

4 Add blocks to change the soloist's costume, play the note and switch the costume back again. Adding the *note* variable into the **play note** block means we can get the soloist to play a different note by just changing the variable *note* before we send the pico-sing message. If you're using Scratch 1.4, change the costume names from pico-b to fantasy1-a, and from pico-a to fantasy1-b

5 Click the cat sprite and drag these blocks into your **forever** block. On the Raspberry Pi use the **broadcast and wait** block because the Pi doesn't cope well with the soloist singing multiple notes at once

6 Click the green flag and test that your soloist sings when you press the **Q** key on the keyboard

7 Return to the Scripts Area for your cat sprite. Duplicate the last blocks you added, and change the key detected to **w** and the value of the *note* variable to 48

8 Repeat the process, adding the keyboard controls for each key on the top row of the keyboard. The keys and corresponding note numbers are:

- q – 48
- w – 50
- e – 52
- r – 53
- t – 55

- y – 57
- u – 59
- i – 60
- o – 62
- p – 64

Hot tip

The notes we've used are a simple scale, but the note numbers don't always go up by the same amount. If you look at a piano, you can see why. Our scale is the white notes (from left to right), and not all the white notes have black notes between them. The next white note has a pitch two higher than the previous one if there's a black note between them. If not, it's just one higher.

Hot tip

You can change the instrument number to change what your soloist sounds like.

Adding a title screen

The Stage can have multiple pictures, in the same way that sprites have costumes. Switch between them to make a title screen:

1 Click the Stage beside the Sprite List, and then click the **Backdrops** tab (in Scratch 2.0, below left) or the **Backgrounds** tab (in Scratch 1.4, below right)

2 This works in the same way as the Costumes Area for sprites. You can duplicate the moon background by right-clicking it in Scratch 2.0, or clicking the **Copy** button in Scratch 1.4. Then you can add the titles using the Paint Editor

3 Alternatively, right-click the moon background and choose to **save to a local file** (Scratch 2.0) or **export this costume**. That will save a copy of the moon background on your computer, so you can edit it with your preferred art program, as I have (above). You can upload the title screen afterwards by clicking the **Upload backdrop from file** button in Scratch 2.0 or the **Import** button in Scratch 1.4. Both are at the top of the Backdrops/Backgrounds Area. In Scratch 2.0, the button is represented by an icon of a folder with an arrow pointing out of it

4 Click the text box above the Paint Editor in Scratch 2.0 or beside the small picture of the title screen in Scratch 1.4. Change the name of the new image to Title Screen

Enabling the title screen

Now you've added the title screen image, here's how to use it:

1 Click the Stage beside the Sprite List, and click the **Scripts** tab. Add the script below. Click the **Looks** button above the Blocks Palette to find the blocks to change the backdrop (in Scratch 2.0, below left) or background (in Scratch 1.4, below right). Create a new broadcast of "start game" that will tell the sprites when the title screen has finished

Hot tip

Alternatively, in Scratch 2.0, there's a new block called "when backdrop switches to [backdrop name]". It's a hat block, so you can use it to start scripts automatically when the Stage switches to the moon backdrop. You'll still need to use a "when green flag clicked" script to hide the sprites while the player is looking at the title screen.

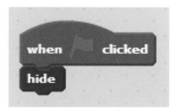

2 Click your cat sprite in the Sprite List and replace its **when green flag clicked** block with a **when I receive [message]** block, and change the message in it to "start game". To remove the top block in a stack, you need to pull the second block away from it

3 Add a new script that hides the sprite when the green flag is clicked. This will keep your sprite hidden while the Stage is showing the title screen

4 Repeat Steps 2 and 3 for all your other sprites

Making your own tunes

You can use what you've learned in this Chapter to write your own music with Scratch, or to write programs that play your favourite tunes. There's lots of sheet music available online for free, and you can use it to work out the numbers you need for your **play note** blocks.

It doesn't matter if you don't know how to read music. You can go a long way by knowing a few basics. The five lines in sheet music are called a stave. Music often has a treble stave (the higher one) and a bass stave (the lower one), and you can tell which is which from the symbol at the start of it. Each spot on the music represents one note, and either sits on a line or in a space. Musicians read the music from left to right. A note's vertical position on the stave tells them its pitch (how high or low the note is), and the shape of the note tells them how long it lasts.

Note names and numbers
Where there is a note displayed in both staves below, one above the other, they represent the same note.

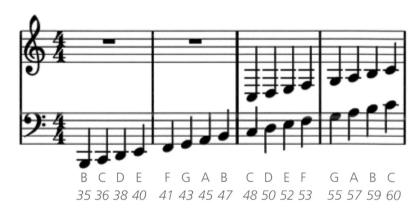

Note durations

As you know, the shape of the notes (whether they're filled or hollow, whether they have a line on them and so on) tells you how many beats the note lasts. If you're using the time signature 4/4 (sometimes shown with a symbol like a large C at the start of the stave), the most common note durations are:

Name	Note length	Duration	Style
semibreve	whole note	4 beats	
minim	half note	2 beats	
crotchet	quarter note	1 beat	
quaver	one-eighth note	0.5 beat	
semiquaver	one-sixteenth note	0.25 beat	

If there's a dot after the note, it's half as long again. So a dotted minim is three beats:

Rests

Music also includes moments of silence, of course, and these are the "rests" between the notes. Here are the symbols you might see for various rests. Remember you can use the **rest for 0.2 beats** block to add these:

Name	Rest length	Duration	Style
semibreve	whole rest	4 beats	
minim	half rest	2 beats	
crotchet	quarter rest	1 beat	
quaver	one-eighth rest	0.5 beat	
semiquaver	one-sixteenth rest	0.25 beat	

London Bridge

Above: The first phrase of the sheet music from the tune. Each note has become one block in the program, making up the first big chunk of purple blocks. I've chosen to play the tune one octave lower because it sounds better.

As an example of how you can make music with Scratch, here's a program that plays the traditional tune "London Bridge is Falling Down". I've also added a slideshow of London photos:

1 Set up your sprite so its costumes include the slides you want to show, and add this script to it to change between them while the program runs

2 The tune includes a bit that repeats. Click the **Data** or **Variables** button above the Blocks Palette and make the variable *verse*. Our program uses this to remember whether it's the first or second time it's gone around its loop. The first time, it plays six additional notes

3 To play the tune, add the script (right) to your sprite

4 Click the green flag button to hear the tune and see the slideshow. When the slideshow reaches the end, it will go back to the beginning and show the first slide again

5 You can customize this program with your own photos, change the instrument played to something else, and try experimenting with different notes

6 Quiz Break

Can you beat the clock? In Quiz Break, you are challenged to answer 10 maths questions in an average of three seconds each. If you do it, the quizmaster does a breakdance. In this project, you'll learn how to use the timer, how to ask the player questions and how to join text in speech bubbles.

Introducing Quiz Break

In recent years, games based on speed maths have become popular on handheld consoles. They're a good warm-up for your brain, as well as being itchingly, frustratingly good fun.

In the game Quiz Break, you're challenged to answer simple maths questions against the clock. If you can answer 10 questions quickly enough, your host will be so impressed he'll breakdance for you. You don't get that on TV quiz shows.

In this chapter, you'll learn how to:

- Ask the player questions

- Use a timer to measure how long the player is taking

- Use the Operators blocks to perform calculations, including calculating an average

- Join pieces of text together so you can make sprites say more complex sentences in their speech bubbles

To complete this project, you'll draw on what you've learned in previous chapters, including using the pen (see Chapter 2), random numbers (see Chapter 4), multiple costumes (see Chapter 5), broadcasts (see Chapter 5), and variables (see Chapter 3).

Hot tip

This game is set up to test your multiplication tables, but you can easily make it test addition, subtraction or division by changing the Operator blocks used.

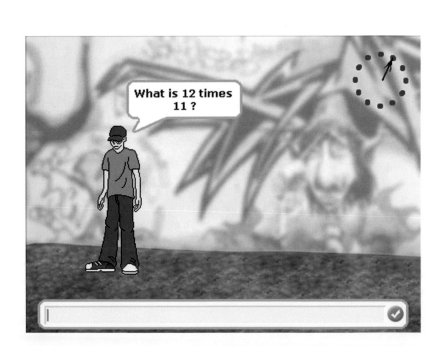

Preparing for Quiz Break

To get ready to make this game, follow these steps:

1 Start a new project and add the graffiti backdrop. It's in the Outdoors category or folder

2 Add the sprite Breakdancer1 in Scratch 2.0, or breakdancer-1 in Scratch 1.4. He's in the People category or folder. He's wearing an orange t-shirt

Hot tip

In Scratch 2.0, the breakdancer sprite includes extra costumes already.

3 If you're using Scratch 1.4, add breakdancer-2, breakdancer-3 and breakdancer-4 as extra costumes on the same sprite. Make sure you pick the costumes with the orange shirt: we want to use these costumes to animate the same sprite, and the illusion won't work if he changes his clothes between each dance move!

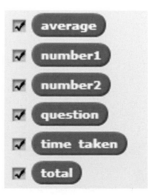

4 Right-click on the cat in the Sprite List and choose **Delete** from the menu. We don't need the cat in this game

5 Click the **Data** or **Variables** button above the Blocks Palette and make six variables with the following names: *average*, *number1*, *number2*, *question*, *time taken*, and *total*. Set them all up to be used by the breakdancer sprite only, except for *time taken*, which must be set up for all sprites

Beware

Make sure time taken is set up for all sprites, otherwise the timer won't work later. The other variables are only needed by the breakdancer sprite for its calculations.

6 Add the sound human beatbox1 (in the Music Loops category in Scratch 2.0) or laugh-male1 (in the Human folder Scratch 1.4) to your breakdancer sprite

7 Your Stage should look like the picture below. In Scratch 1.4, the breakdancer sprite is called Sprite2 and might be in a different pose

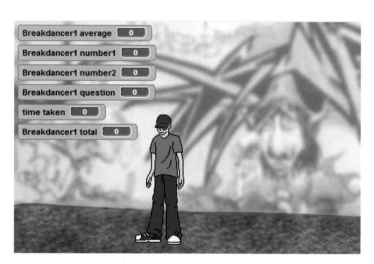

8 At the start of the game, you need to hide the variables on the Stage, switch to the costume that shows the dancer standing upright, and move the breakdancer to the left of the Stage. Add the script shown to the breakdancer. In Scratch 2.0, the starting costume name is breakdancer1-c (as shown in the script), but in Scratch 1.4, it's breakdancer-1

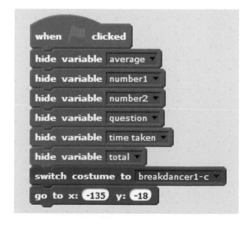

Drawing the timer

To pile on the pressure and give players a visual clue as to how well they're doing, let's add a clock in the top-right corner:

1 In Scratch 2.0, add the Arrow2 sprite, which is in the Things category of the Sprite Library. In Scratch 1.4, add the sprite Clock-hand in the Things folder

2 To draw the outline of the clock, let's use the pen on the arrow or clock hand sprite. Click the sprite in the Sprite List to make sure you're adding your script to the right sprite

3 The sprite in Scratch 1.4 comes with a script already. Some of these blocks will come in handy later so you can keep them in the Scripts Area, but you don't want them to be activated when the green flag is clicked. Click the second block and drag it away from the **when green flag clicked** block

Hot tip

If you're using Scratch 1.4, try clicking the green flag before you split apart the script in Step 3.

4 Add the following blocks to the sprite. They position the sprite in the top-right corner of the Stage, and set the pen size. They also set the starting direction as 15 degrees, which ensures the spots line up with the clock points

Above: The clock face looks wonky if you start drawing with the arrow pointing up, down, left or right. That's because the arrow starts drawing in the middle of the clock point. Use a starting angle of 15 degrees to fix this.

Don't forget

You can have more than one script on a sprite. In this game, we'll have two scripts on the clock hand: one that is activated when the green flag is clicked, and one that starts the hand moving when the game begins.

5 To make the twelve spots on the clock face, draw a dotted dodecagon (a twelve sided shape). Using a thick pen, you can take one step with the pen down to leave a spot, and then move several steps with the pen up to add spacing between the dots. Because we're making 12 spots, we need to turn 30 degrees after each one (30 x 12 = 360 degrees, which completes the circle). Add these blocks to your script (right)

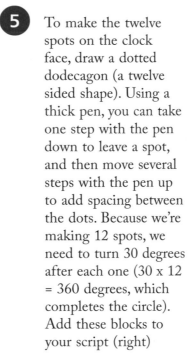

6 To finish, position the arrow in the middle of the clock face (at x:192 y:125) and point it in direction 0, which is up, towards the 12 o'clock position. Add these blocks underneath your repeat loop

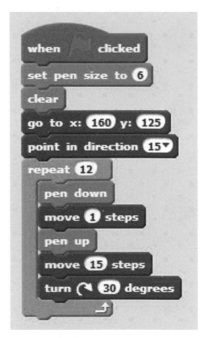

7 Finally, add a block to adjust the size of the sprite. In Scratch 2.0, set the size to 50%, as shown. In Scratch 1.4, set the size to 15%

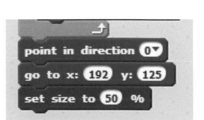

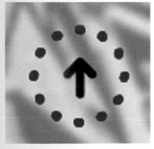

Above: The finished clock in Scratch 2.0. In Scratch 1.4, the clock hand will look different, but the clock will otherwise be the same.

Moving the clock hand

Scratch has a timer built in to it, and there are two Sensing blocks you can use to work with it:

- **reset timer**: This block sets the timer to zero. In Scratch 2.0, the timer is also set to zero when the green flag is clicked. In Scratch 1.4, the timer is reset when a new project is opened or created, but the timer keeps running until you reset it.

- **timer**: You can use this block to see how many seconds have passed since the timer was reset. The block is like a variable that you can't change, and you can use it in place of a number in another block. Even after you've clicked the **Stop** button above the Stage, the timer keeps running.

To animate the clock hands, follow these steps:

1   Click your Arrow or Clock Hand sprite in the Sprite List, and add the **when I receive [message]** block. In Scratch 2.0, it's an Events block. In Scratch 1.4, it's a Control block. Click the menu in the block and create a new message called "start clock". Our breakdancer will send this message to start the clock ticking

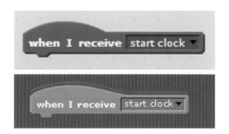

Don't forget

Click the Sensing button above the Blocks Palette to find the timing blocks.

2   Add the **reset timer** block to your script, so the clock always starts with a value of zero, which will translate into the clock hand pointing upwards

3   Add the **repeat until** Control block to your script

...cont'd

4 We'll use the variable *time taken* to measure how long the player took to answer 10 questions. The clock can use this variable to tell whether the game has finished or not, because its value will be zero until the game ends, and then it will be a number higher than zero. Click the **Operators** button above the Blocks Palette and drag the > block into the diamond-shaped hole in your **repeat until** block

5 Click the **Data** or **Variables** button above the Blocks Palette. Drag the *time taken* variable block into the left of your Operator block. Type a number 0 at the right

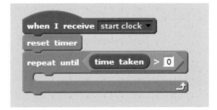

Don't forget
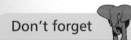

The > block is used to check whether the number or variable on the left is higher than the number or variable on the right.

6 Inside the bracket of the **repeat until** block, add the **point in direction 90** block

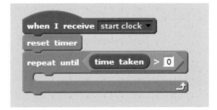

7 Now, you need to change this block so it points the sprite in the right direction, depending on the timer value. The direction is calculated by multiplying the timer (measured in seconds) by 6. That's because we want the hand to do a full circle (360 degrees) in a minute and there are 60 seconds in a minute. (60 x 6 = 360). Click the **Operators** button above the Blocks Palette and drag the rounded block with an asterisk in it into the **point in direction 90** block. The * means multiply

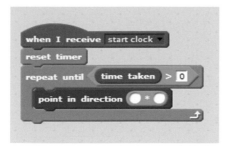

Hot tip

Tick the box beside the "timer" block in the Blocks Palette, and you can see the value of the timer on the Stage. When you're writing a program that uses the timer, this can help you to find out what's causing any errors you experience.

123

8 Click the **Sensing** button above the Blocks Palette and drag the **timer** block into one of the holes in your multiplication operator. Type a 6 into the other hole

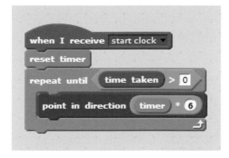

9 Although this script uses a broadcast to trigger it, you can test it by double-clicking it in the Scripts Area. You should see the hand on your clock turn around, like the second hand on a clock

Adding a rising sound effect

To ratchet up the tension, add a sound effect to the clock that gets higher with every passing second:

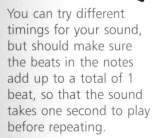

Hot tip

You can try different timings for your sound, but should make sure the beats in the notes add up to a total of 1 beat, so that the sound takes one second to play before repeating.

1 Add the **set instrument** and **set tempo** blocks between your hat block and your **reset timer** block

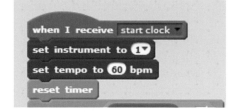

2 Choose your favorite instrument, and make sure the tempo is set to 60. That means there are 60 beats per minute, or one per second

3 Drag two **play note** blocks into your **repeat until** loop

4 There is another Operator block that adds two numbers together, with a + sign in it. Drag it into one of the **play note** blocks in place of the note number

Hot tip

Instead of playing a specific note, we're playing the value of a variable here, the timer, and we're adding it to our starting note. As time passes, the note number played is greater and so the tone gets higher. Look out for opportunities like this in your own programs to create sound effects that change as the game is played. You could try playing a sprite's position using the x position or y position Motion blocks, or perhaps play your score variable.

5 Click the **Sensing** button above the Blocks Palette and drag the **timer** block into one side of your addition Operator block. In the other side, type 36

6 Change the note in the other **play note** block to 36. Tweak the timings, so the first note plays for 0.75 beats and the second one plays for 0.25 beats

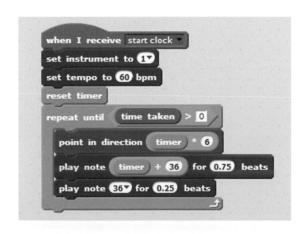

Asking questions

If you want to ask the player a question, there are two Sensing blocks you can use:

- **ask [What's your name?] and wait**: When you use this block, a box opens at the bottom of the screen for the player to type something into, and the stack of blocks it is in pauses until the player enters something. The player can finish typing by pressing the Enter key on the keyboard, or clicking the tick on the right of the box. The question is shown in a speech bubble and you can change it to anything you like.

- **answer**: After the player has typed something in, this block contains the answer. The information in this block is emptied when the green flag is clicked. When another question is asked, the old answer is replaced by the new answer.

When you ask a question, it looks like this:

One thing to beware of is that if you ask a question, you'll lose the answer to a previous question, unless you've stored it in a variable. You can do that by using the **set [variable] to 0** block, and dragging the answer block into the space where the 0 is. Variables can store text as well as numbers, so it doesn't matter what information you're saving for later. Using the blocks here, for example, you can store the player's name in the *name* variable so you can use it again later if you need to.

Beware

The "ask" block only pauses the stack of blocks it is in. Other scripts continue to run, so the clock hand keeps moving while the breakdancer waits for the player to answer a question.

125

Don't forget

You can find the block to set the variable in the Data or Variables section of the Blocks Palette. You need to make a variable before you can use it. To find the "ask" and "answer" blocks, click the Sensing button above the Blocks Palette.

Joining text to greet players

When the game starts, let's ask the player their name and then say hello to them. This isn't quite as simple as it might seem:

1 Click the breakdancer sprite in the Sprite List

2 Click the **Sensing** button above the Blocks Palette and drag the **ask [What's your name?] and wait** block into the Scripts Area and join it to your script so far

3 Click the **Looks** button above the Blocks Palette and add two **say Hello! for 2 secs** blocks

4 Click the **Sensing** button above the Blocks Palette and drag the **answer** block into the space for text in the second **say** block

5 Click the green flag to try it. When you enter your name, the breakdancer will say hello to you (in a speech bubble) and then say your name in another speech bubble. It would be better if we could greet the player using one speech bubble, and include their name in it

6 To do that, click the **Operators** button above the Blocks Palette and drag in the **join hello world** block. This block is used for joining two bits of text together. Put it into the Hello! space in your first **say** block

7 Drag the **answer** block into the second half of the **join** block. The first half can stay as "hello"

8 Drag your second **say** block into the Blocks Palette to remove it, then click the green flag again. Much better!

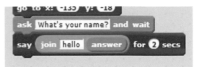

Hot tip

In programming, bits of text are often called strings.

Hot tip

It's important to be able to join pieces of text like this, otherwise you'll need five speech bubbles to ask the player one maths question!

Above: By using the "join hello world" operator, you can combine two bits of text in one speech bubble. Here we've combined the word "hello", and the name the player entered.

Preparing the quiz

You should have a clock that's ready to tick, and a breakdancer who asks the player's name and greets them with a friendly hello. Now let's build the main part of the game. Add these blocks to your script for the breakdancer so far:

1 With timing-based games like this, it's only fair to make sure the player is ready before you start. To do this, tell the player to tap the Space key to start, and use a **wait until** block that pauses until the space key is pressed. The **wait until** block is a Control block and the **key space pressed?** block is a Sensing block

Don't forget

We're using the "say" block and not the "say for 2 Secs" block here. Using the "say" block without a time limit keeps the message on screen until the sprite says something else.

2 Set the *time taken* variable to 0 and then broadcast the "start clock" message. The clock hand will start moving when it receives the "start clock" message, and it will keep going until the *time taken* variable is changed to something higher than zero

Don't forget

In Scratch 2.0, the broadcast blocks are Events blocks and in Scratch 1.4, they are Control blocks.

3 There are 10 questions in the quiz, so add a **repeat 10** block

Making the questions

Now you're ready to add the blocks that will create the questions:

1 Each quiz question will ask the player to multiply two numbers chosen at random. We'll put one of those numbers into the variable *number1* and the other one into the variable *number2*. Add two **set [variable] to 0** blocks inside your **repeat** bracket. Change the variable in one to *number1*, and the other to *number2*

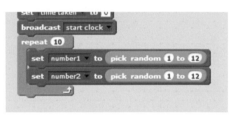

2 Click the **Operators** button above the Blocks Palette and drag the **pick random 1 to 10** block into the **set number1** and **set number2** blocks. Change the second number in it to 12, so we're testing the full multiplication table

3 We're going to use the *question* variable to store our question, which will look something like "What is 5 times 9?" The actual numbers are the random numbers we put into the *number1* and *number2* variables a moment ago. We're going to build the question up using the **join hello world** block, so start by setting the question to be "What is " (with a space at the end) joined to the variable *number1*. The **set [variable name]** block is a Data or Variables block, and the **join hello world** block is an Operators block

128

4 The next step is to add the word **"times"** (with a space either side of it) to the

question variable. To do this set the variable to be itself joined to the word "times"

5 Repeat that process to add *number2* to the *question* variable. Add a question mark at the end

6 Click the **Sensing** button above the Blocks Palette and drag in **ask [What's your name?] and wait**

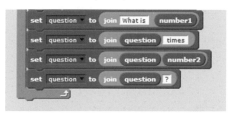

7 Click the **Data** or **Variables** button and drag the variable *question* into the **ask** block

8 Click the green flag to test it! You should be asked 10 random multiplication questions. The game doesn't check your answers yet, though

What is 4 times 12?

Don't forget

You can save time by duplicating the block you make in Step 4 repeatedly and using it in Step 5.

129

Beware

Everything relating to asking and answering questions goes inside the repeat loop. It happens 10 times because there are 10 random questions.

Checking the answers

After the player enters a number, we need to check whether it is right or not. The following blocks are added underneath your blocks so far, but are still inside the bracket of the **repeat 10** block:

1 First, let's calculate the correct answer and store it in the variable *total*. Click the **Data** or **Variables** button above the Blocks Palette. Add the **set [variable] to 0** block to your script. Set the variable name to *total*

2 Click the **Operators** button above the Blocks Palette. Add the multiplication operator in your **set total** block

3 Click the **Data** or **Variables** button above the Blocks Palette. Drag the *number1* and *number2* variables into each side of the multiplication Operator block

4 Click the **Control** button above the Blocks Palette and add an **if... then... else** block

5 We want to check whether one number (the player's answer) is equal to another number (the right answer, stored in the variable *total*). Click the **Operators** button above the Blocks Palette and drag the = block into the diamond-shaped hole in the **if...then...else** block

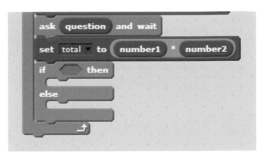

6   Click the **Sensing** button above the Blocks Palette and drag the **answer** block into the = block

7   Click the **Data** or **Variables** button above the Blocks Palette and drag the variable *total* into the = block

8   The **if...then...else** block has two brackets. The first one contains blocks that should run if whatever we're checking for is true, so in this case, if the answer entered matches the right answer. Click the **Looks** button above the Blocks Palette and drag a **say Hello! for 2 secs** block into the first bracket. Change the message in it to **Correct!** and the timing to 0.5 seconds

9   Drag another **say Hello! for 2 secs** block into the second bracket. Change the message in it to **That's not right!** and the timing to 5 seconds

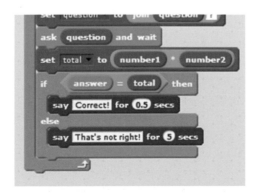

Hot tip

If the player gets it right, the game moves quickly on to the next question. If not, there's a 5-second delay before the next question, so the player suffers a time penalty.

Reporting the scores

Success in this game is measured by the time taken to answer the questions, the faster the better. When the player has been asked 10 questions, you need to report the scores:

 Add the **set [variable name] to 0** block to your script. You've finished asking your 10 questions now, so join this block underneath your **repeat 10** block, not inside it. Change the variable name to *time taken*

 Drag the **timer** Sensing block into your **set [variable name]** block. The timer will keep on ticking, but the variable stores its value in this variable as soon as the player has answered your 10 questions. Remember that the clock hand stops moving when the *time taken* variable changes

 Add another **set [variable name]** block to your script. Change the variable name to *average*. The average is calculated by dividing the *time taken* variable by 10, because there are 10 questions. To divide one number by another you use the / Operator block, which divides the first number by the second number

 Add two **show variable** blocks into your script and change the variable names in them to *time taken* and *average*, to show the final scores on the Stage

Adding the victory dance

If the player answers all 10 questions quickly enough, the quizmaster does a breakdance for them:

1 Add an **if...then...else** block to your script

2 We want to check whether the average time taken is less than our target of three seconds, so click the **Operators** button above the Blocks Palette and drag the < block into the diamond-shaped hole in your **if...then...else** block

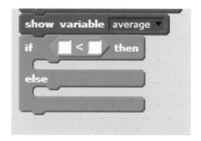

3 Click the **Data** or **Variables** button above the Blocks Palette and drag the **average** block into the left of the < block. Type a number 3 into the right of it

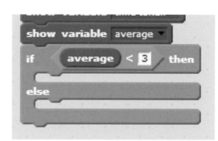

4 The first bracket of the **if...then...else** block is used for blocks that should run when the average time is less than three, so this is where we put our dance. Click the **Sounds** button above the Blocks Palette and drag in the block to play the human beatbox or laugh sound effect

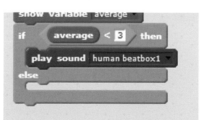

5 Add a **repeat 10** block and change the number in it to 9

Don't forget

The < block checks whether the number on the left is less than the number on the right.

Hot tip

If the average time of three seconds is too fast for you, use a bigger number instead. Remember, though: If you can beat it every time, it's not challenging enough!

Hot tip

Our dance routine repeats nine times because each dance pose takes half a second and the soundtrack plays for about 4.5 seconds.

...cont'd

6 Click the **Looks** button above the Blocks Palette and drag the **next costume** block into the bracket of your **repeat** block. It changes a sprite to its next costume, and when it runs out, goes back to the first one again

7 Add a **wait 1 secs** Control block, again inside your repeat bracket, and change the time in it to 0.5 seconds

8 When the dance finishes, we need to switch the dancer back to his upright costume of breakdancer1-c (or breakdancer-1 in Scratch 1.4). Add the **switch costume** Looks block. This

belongs outside the **repeat 9** bracket (because we only want to do it once), but inside the **if** bracket (because it's still part of the victory dance)

9 Drag the **say Hello! for 2 secs** block into the other bracket of your **if...then...else** block. This is for when the player doesn't beat the clock, so add an encouraging message to invite them to try again

Above: The breakdancing sprites in Scratch 1.4. Scratch 2.0 has only three of these costumes.

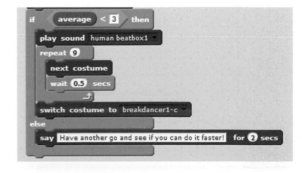

7 Hangman

Create the classic word game Hangman, and you'll learn how to structure more sophisticated projects using broadcasts, how to use lists to manage information, how to use graphic effects with your sprites, and how to write on the Stage with a sprite. You can personalize this game with your own choice of word lists and your choice of cartoon host.

Introducing Hangman

In this traditional game, you have to guess the letters that could be in a mystery word. If you guess correctly, you're shown where your guessed letter appears in the word. If you guess wrongly, another stroke is drawn on the gallows, and when that drawing's finished, it's game over.

This is a one player game, with the computer randomly picking a word from a list, and telling you whether your guesses are right or wrong. The game might seem simple, but implementing it in Scratch will draw on most of your skills so far.

In particular, you'll need to use the blocks for asking questions that were introduced last chapter, and the broadcast blocks you first met in Chapter 5. You'll also learn how to:

- Store lists of information, such as lists of words

- Write text on the Stage using a sprite

- Look at individual letters in a piece of text

- Use broadcasts to create programs that are easier to read, and easier to write

- Use graphic effects with your sprites

Hot tip

Of course, if you're writing the program, you'll know the words in it! But if you make the list long enough, you might forget the words, or you could get a friend to add some words to the program for you.

Importing the images

Before you can start programming, get your pictures ready. This is quite an involved process, because you'll need an image for each stage of the gallows and an image for each letter of the alphabet:

1 First, add a background. You'll be putting letters and the gallows illustration on top of it, so make it something simple. I chose the illustrated brick wall in the Outdoors Category of Scratch 2.0, and the Outdoors folder of Scratch 1.4

2 Add a sprite to use as the game host. If you're using Scratch 2.0, add the Dinosaur1 sprite in the Animals category, because he has seven costumes with some great expressions to choose from

3 If you're using Scratch 1.4, I recommend adding the quizzical sprite dog2-a, and add dog2-b as an additional costume. Don't worry about missing out on the dinosaur. You'll get your revenge on Scratch 2.0 in a minute when you make the alphabet sprite!

137

Hot tip

You could use any sprites and backgrounds you like for this. How about an underwater background, with a fish asking the questions? Or a ghost at a castle? When you add words later, you could theme them too, using the names of fish or castles, for example.

Hot tip

You don't need the cat, so you can delete it from this project.

Making the gallows

1 Click the button to paint a new sprite

2 This first costume represents the blank page before the first line is drawn. In Scratch 1.4, you can't make a blank costume, so draw the smallest dot you can. We'll use a **hide** block, but your sprite will still be seen for a moment

3 Click the **Costumes** tab and click the button to paint a new costume. For this one, draw a thick horizontal line

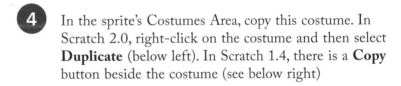

4 In the sprite's Costumes Area, copy this costume. In Scratch 2.0, right-click on the costume and then select **Duplicate** (below left). In Scratch 1.4, there is a **Copy** button beside the costume (see below right)

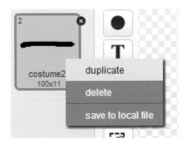 

5 If you're using Scratch 1.4, click the **Edit** button beside this new copy

6 Add the next line of the gallows: a vertical line that turns your first line into an L shape

7 Repeat the process until you've drawn the complete gallows. You should have your empty first costume plus 11 costumes. The costumes look like this

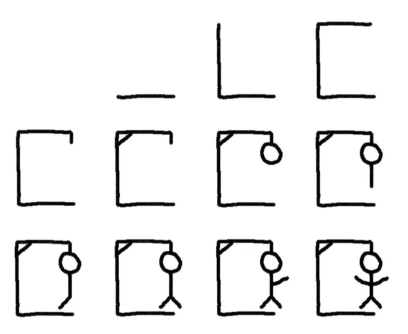

Don't forget

Chapter 4 taught you how to use the Paint Editor to make your own sprites. Flick back to it if you need a reminder.

8 Change the name of your first costume to "empty". In Scratch 2.0 (left, below), click the costume and edit its name above the Paint Editor. In Scratch 1.4, edit its name in the text box in the Costumes Area (right, below)

Making the alphabet sprite

There isn't a built-in way in Scratch to write letters on the Stage. To get around this, you can use a sprite with a costume for each letter of the alphabet, change it to the letter you want, and then stamp it on the Stage. As well as the letters A to Z, you need a costume with a question mark in it, which you'll use to indicate the unguessed letters in the word.

The process of making the sprite is simple, but time consuming!

1 Click the button above the Sprite List to paint a new sprite. Draw a letter A

2 Click the button to paint a new costume and draw a letter B. Repeat this step for the rest of the alphabet

3 Add a final costume which is a question mark. You should have a total of 27 costumes

Adding letters from files in Scratch 1.4

Alternatively, you could add the letter costumes from files. In Scratch 1.4, the Sprite Library includes costumes for letters of the alphabet. Follow these steps:

1 Click the button above the Sprite List to open a new sprite from the Sprite Library

2 Double-click the Letters folder. There are 10 folders to choose from, each one containing a different letter style. Double-click the outline folder

3 Double-click the letter A to add it as a sprite

4 Click the **Import** button and add the letter B. Repeat this step to add the rest of the alphabet

Creating the variables

We're going to use a lot of variables in this game. Click the **Data** or the **Variables** button above the Blocks Palette and then click the **Make a Variable** button to make the following variables.

Some variables are needed only by one sprite (*score* is only used by the dinosaur or dog sprite, and *word marker* is only used by the letter sprite), but others are needed by all sprites. To avoid the complexity of clicking between the sprites to set up different variables for them, set up all the variables to work on all sprites:

- *alphabet*: This variable stores the alphabet, and is used for writing the guessed letters on the Stage.

- *gameover status*: This variable stores the value PLAYING, LOST or WON, depending on the status of the game.

- *letter guessed*: This stores the letter the player entered.

- *score*: This records how many letters the player has correctly guessed.

- *was guess right*: This variable is used when the program checks whether a guess was right or not, to keep track of whether the guessed letter was in the word anywhere.

- *word to guess*: This is the word the player is trying to figure out. It will be randomly chosen at the start of the game.

- *word length*: This variable stores the length of the word the player is trying to guess. When the player's score matches the word length, they've won.

Additionally, these variables are used by different **repeat** loops to keep track of how many times we've been around the loop:

- *alphabet marker*

- *letter marker*

- *word marker*

Hot tip

It's okay to experiment with your programs to see what works and what doesn't. I tried making this game another way at first, using a different sprite for each letter in the word. It was clumsy synchronizing between the sprites, so I worked out this simpler solution.

141

Don't forget

When you add a variable, it's shown on the Stage. Untick the box beside the variable name in the Blocks Palette to hide it again. With so many variables, the Stage will be half covered with them otherwise.

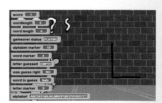

Setting up the gallows

The gallows sprite is the easiest one to understand, so let's start by setting it up:

Hot tip

You can test these scripts by clicking them in the Scripts Area to run them.

1 When the game starts, you need to put the gallows on the right of the Stage and switch to the first costume, which represents the blank page before the first stroke is drawn. Because Scratch 1.4 won't let you add a blank costume, we'll also **hide** it. Click your gallows sprite in the Sprite List, click the **Scripts** tab, and build this script (right)

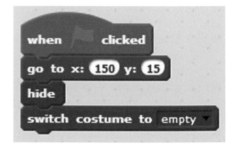

Hot tip

Because the first costume (the empty page) is a different size to the others (the gallows), you need to put your "set size" block after the costume change.

2 Each time the player guesses a wrong letter, the broadcast "wrong guess" will tell the gallows sprite to advance to its next costume. Drag the **when I receive [message]** block into the Scripts Area. Click the menu and create a new message for "wrong guess"

Don't forget

The blocks for broadcasting and receiving messages are brown Events blocks in Scratch 2.0, but they're yellow Control blocks in Scratch 1.4.

3 You hid the sprite when the game started to make sure the game began with a blank space where the gallows will be, so you need to use a **show** block to bring it back. I've also added a block to adjust the size of my gallows to fit comfortably: you might or might not need to do the same, depending on how big your pictures are. The **next costume** block appears to draw another line on the gallows

Losing the game

The gallows sprite is also where we will check whether the player has lost the game. We don't need to use a variable to keep track of how many wrong guesses the player has made, because there is a Looks block that tells us which costume number the gallows is on. When it reaches number 12, the game ends:

1 Click the **Control** button above the Blocks Palette and drag an **if** block in to join your script for the wrong guess

2 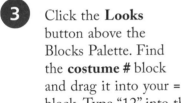 You want to check whether the costume number is equal to 12, so click the **Operators** button above the Blocks Palette and drag the = block into the diamond shaped hole in your **if** block

Don't forget

In Scratch 2.0, the "if" block says "then" on it. In Scratch 1.4, it doesn't.

3 Click the **Looks** button above the Blocks Palette. Find the **costume #** block and drag it into your = block. Type "12" into the other side of the = block

4 If the costume number is 12, the player has lost the game, so you need to change the variable *gameover status* to LOST. Our main script will use this to know it shouldn't ask for any more guesses, and should tell the player they've lost, and what the answer was. Click the **Data** or **Variables** button above the Blocks Palette and drag in the **set [variable] to 0** block. Click the menu in the block to pick the *gameover status* variable, and type **LOST** into the box

Hot tip

The "costume #" block is at the bottom in Scratch 2.0. Use the scrollbar on the right edge of the Blocks Palette to find it.

Beware

The graphic effects can be quite slow on the Raspberry Pi. If you're using Scratch 1.4 and want Pi fans to play your game, avoid using graphic effects in any parts of your game that repeat a lot.

Hot tip

It's worth playing around with the graphic effects to see how you can use them in your programs.

Adding graphic effects

Scratch includes a number of graphic effects you can apply to the background and your sprites. They are:

- **color,** which changes the sprite's color palette

- **fisheye**, which distorts like a fisheye camera lens, with central parts of the image being magnified

- **whirl**, which twists the picture around its middle, like water circling a drain

- **pixelate**, which makes the picture blockier

- **mosaic**, which turns the image into lots of small tiles of itself

- **brightness,** which adjusts the brightness of the sprite's colors

- **ghost**, which makes the sprite semi-transparent

Three blocks are used to manage these effects. You can find them all in the Looks section of the Blocks Palette:

- **change color effect by 25**: Click the menu in the block to change the effect from color to one of the others. Click to edit the number. You can use negative numbers too

- **set color effect to 0**: This block resets the chosen effect

- **clear graphic effects**: This block resets all graphic effects

Right: Showing the color effects. The brightness effect is using a negative number here to darken the sprite.

...cont'd

You can make your game look more interesting by adding some graphic effects to the gallows sprite:

1 Click the gallows sprite in the Sprite List. Click the **Looks** button above the Blocks Palette and drag in the **set color effect to 0** block. Put it above your **next costume** block. Click the menu in the block and choose **ghost**. Change the number in the block to 50. This makes your sprite semi-transparent, so

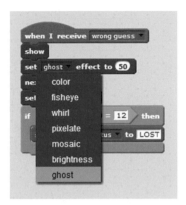

it looks like the gallows are drawn on the wall, with the brickwork showing through

Hot tip

Why change the effect 10 times, instead of just changing it once by -250, and then again by 250? Using a loop makes the effect appear to happen gradually, rather than the sprite just snapping out of shape and then back in again.

2 Click the **Control** button above the Blocks Palette and drag in a **repeat 10** block, immediately above your **next costume** block

3 Click the **Looks** button above the Blocks Palette and drag the **change color effect by 25** block into your **repeat** bracket.

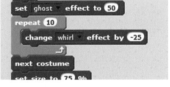

Click the menu to change the effect to **whirl**. Change the number in the **change whirl effect** block to -25

Hot tip

If you reduce an effect by 250, and then increase it by 250, you end up back where you started. But the effect looks like the gallows are stretching and morphing to add new lines, which looks great!

4 Repeat Step 3, but this time put the **repeat 10** block after your **next costume** and **set size** blocks, and leave the number in the effect block as 25

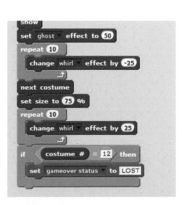

5 Click your stack of blocks to see it working

Creating the main script

As programs become longer, it's important to make sure they're well organized, so you can easily understand which bits do what. One way to do that is to split your program into smaller sections and use broadcasts to coordinate between them. The advantages of this approach are:

- If you use meaningful names for your broadcasts, it becomes easy to see what each bit of program does, so you can easily find and fix any errors.

- To replace a part of the program, you can just move the **when I receive [message]** block to a different stack of blocks.

- To test part of it, you can click a script to run it, without having to first separate it from the rest of the program.

- You can reuse bits of a program by just broadcasting the message that triggers them more than once.

The main game script manages the overall flow of the game and using broadcasts makes it much easier to understand:

Hot tip

Scratch 2.0 introduced the ability to make your own blocks, which can also help you to write structured programs. See Ransom Writer in Chapter 10.

Hot tip

By using the broadcast block with the wait on it, we guarantee the variables and board are ready before we go any further.

Hot tip

Apart from the script that resets the gallows, this is the only script activated by the green flag in this game.

1. Click your dinosaur, dog or other lead sprite in the Sprite List

2. Drag these blocks into the Scripts Area. The **clear** block gets rid of any letters and question marks left on the Stage from a previous game

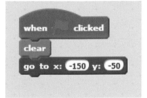

3. Drag two **broadcast [message] and wait** blocks into your script, and click the menu in them to create new broadcasts. Call them "set up variables" and "show board". We'll use these to start scripts that set up the variables used in the game, and to display the game board of guessed and unguessed letters

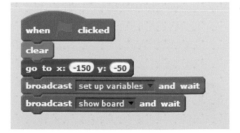

...cont'd

4 The next blocks switch to the excited dinosaur costume, introduce the game with a speech bubble, and set the variable *gameover status* to PLAYING. If you're using a different sprite, choose a suitable starting costume

Above: Our game so far, with a friendly welcome from our Jurassic friend.

5 The blocks so far set the game up. The next step is to create the main game loop. This should repeat until the game is either won or lost. Drag in a **repeat until** block, and add the **or** Operator block in it

147

6 We're going to check whether the variable *gameover status* is set to WON or LOST, so we need two = Operator blocks

Beware

Take care adding the "=" blocks. Wait until the space in the "or" block is glowing before releasing the mouse button, otherwise your "=" block might replace the "or" block instead of going inside it.

7 Drag the variable *gameover status* into one side of each of the = blocks. Write WON in the other half of one of them, and LOST in the other half

...cont'd

8 Add two new **broadcast and wait** blocks inside the loop. Create new messages called "player inputs letter" and "check the letter"

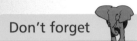
9 Finally, add a broadcast block after the loop and set the message in it to "game over"

10 The final main script is shown below. The flow of the program is that we set up the variables, show the game board, greet the player, and then enter the main game loop. This loop gets the player to enter a letter and then checks the letter to see if it's in the word. This will keep going until the game's status changes from PLAYING to WON or LOST. When it does, it's game over

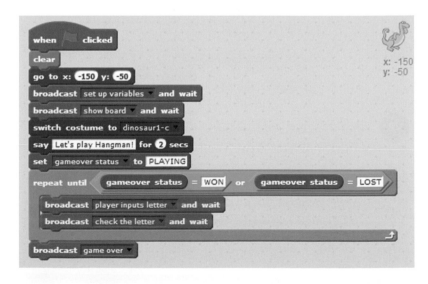

Creating lists

As well as variables, Scratch gives you another way to store information, which is in a list. A list is perfect for organizing similar items, such as numbers in a high-score table or words in a quiz game. We'll use three lists in Hangman: one for the pool of words that the mystery word is taken from, one for the game board, and one to remember the letters the player has guessed so we can stop them guessing the same letter twice.

To create a list, follow these steps:

1 Click the **Data** button above the Blocks Palette in Scratch 2.0, or the **Variables** button above the Blocks Palette in Scratch 1.4

2 Click the **Make a List** button. A box opens, like the one used to make a variable

3 Enter the name for the list in the box. We'll need a list called *game board* for Hangman, so enter this name now.
The *game board* list will be used for the mystery word as seen by the player, a mixture of guessed letters and question marks marking unguessed ones

4 As with variables, you can make a list for all sprites or just for one sprite. Check that this list will be available to all sprites

5 Repeat these steps to make a new list, this time called *word list*, and another called *guessed letters*

6 As with a variable, lists are displayed on the Stage when they're created. They take up much more room, though. Untick the box beside each list name in the blocks palette to hide it from the Stage

149

Hot tip

To delete a list or variable in Scratch 2.0, right-click its name in the Blocks Palette and then click delete in the menu. In Scratch 1.4, click the "Delete a variable" or "Delete a list" button in the Variables part of the Blocks Palette.

Hot tip

Displaying lists on the Stage clogs it up and can slow down your program. It's a good idea, then, to only show them if they should be seen by players (such as a list of items being carried in an adventure game), or if you're trying to fix a list-related error.

Using lists

When you make a list in Scratch, it adds a set of blocks to the Data or Variables part of the Blocks Palette, which you can use for managing the list. The new blocks are:

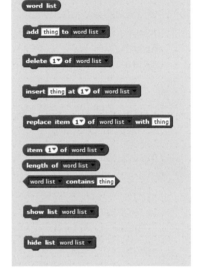

- **add thing to [list name]:** This block adds something to the end of your list. You can type a word or number where it says "thing", or you can drag in a variable or a rounded block like the **x position** or **timer**. With all these blocks, use the menu in the block to choose which list you want to use.

- **delete 1 of [list name]:** This block is used to remove an item from the list. Any items after the deleted item move up the list so there's no gap. If you repeatedly delete the first item, the whole list will eventually disappear. You can use other numbers here (2 for the second item, and so on), or click the menu beside the 1 to choose an option that deletes all of the list or the last item.

- **insert thing at 1 of [list name]:** Use this to insert an item in the list. Any items after the inserted item shuffle further down the list to make room. You can change "thing" to different text, a number or a rounded block, such as a variable. Click the 1 to open a menu with options to insert at the last place or a random place in the list. You can also type another position number or use a variable in place of the 1.

- **replace item 1 of [list name] with thing:** Use this to replace an item in the list with another. You can edit the number to choose a different list item, and can change "thing" to alternative text, a number, or a rounded block. Click the menu beside the 1 to get options to replace the last or a random list item in the list.

- **item 1 of [list name]**: This rounded block is used to get information out of your list again. You could drag it into a **say** block, for example, or set a variable using it. You can change the number, replace it with a variable, or click the menu beside the number to pick the last or a random list item.

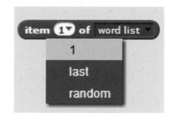

Hot tip

For a short demo of lists, see Penguin Patter in Chapter 10.

- **length of [list name]**: This block is like a variable that always tells you how many items are in the list.

- **[list name] contains thing**: Use this block to see whether "thing", or the text or number you use in the block, is in the list. The block is shaped like a diamond, and you'll most often put it inside an **if** block's frame to make a decision based on whether something's in a list or not. When you add a variable to a list, you actually add the variable's contents. The list doesn't remember which variable the contents came from. Imagine there's a variable called *name* and one called *winner*, and they both have the same text in them. If you add *name* to the list, and then check whether the list contains *winner*, the answer will be yes.

151

- **show list [list name]**: This block will show your list on the Stage, as you can see on the right. When list items are used by your program, the number beside them flashes. When there are too many list items to fit in the box, there is a scroll bar to see more. You can click and drag the bottom right corner of the list box to make it bigger or smaller. The plus button in the bottom left is used to add a new list item. You can also edit the list items in this box.

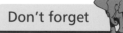
Don't forget

Before you can use these blocks with a list, you must click the Make a List button to create the list. There's no option in the block menu to create the list, as there is with messages for the broadcast related blocks.

- **hide list [list name]**: This block hides your list on the Stage.

Setting up the variables

On the same sprite as your main game loop, add another script which will be used to set up the variables at the start of the game. Because all the blocks that set up variables and lists are in the same small script, it's easy to find them if you need to make any changes later, including adding words to the word list:

1 This script should be triggered when it gets the message "set up variables" so drag the **when I receive [message]** block into your script and click the menu in it to choose this message

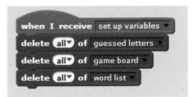

2 Lists aren't cleared when the game ends, so if somebody plays twice, their previously-guessed letters will still be in the list unless we reset them first. Clear all the lists by adding three **delete 1 of [list name]** blocks, clicking the menu beside the 1 to choose **all**, and changing the name to each of your lists

Hot tip

Seeing these blocks tells you the possible right answers in the game. In the downloadable version of this game, I'll change the words from those used here so you can play the game too!

3 Use the **add thing to [list name]** block to add some mystery words to your word list. One of these words will be chosen for the player to guess. I've added five words, but you can make the game more replayable by adding many more

4 The variable *word to guess* will be used to store the word that the player is trying to guess in this run of the game. That word will be picked at random from the list. Drag the **set [variable name] to 0** block into your script and click the menu in the block to choose *word to guess*. Add the **item 1 of [list name]** block into that block's hole, and click the 1 to open the menu and choose **random** or **any** in Scratch 1.4. Change the list name to *word list*

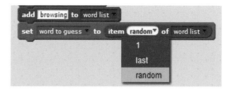

5 We'll store the length of the word in a variable called *word length*. Drag in the **set [variable] to 0** block. Change the variable in it to *word length*. There's an Operator block called **length of world** that can tell you how long any piece of text is. In this block, "world" is just some example text and you can replace it with other text, or more often, a variable. Click the **Operators** button and drag the **length of world** block into your **set variable** block

6 Click the **Data** or **Variables** button above the Blocks Palette and drag the **word to guess** variable into the **length of world** block

...cont'd

7 The list *game board* is used to store what the player sees of the word on screen. At the start of the game, each list item will be a question mark. As the player guesses letters, the question marks will be replaced with those letters. If the player guesses the second letter, for example, the second question mark in the list will be replaced with the right letter. At the start of the game, we need to set this list up so it contains a question mark for each letter. That means it should finish with the same number of items as the length of the word, and each one should be a question mark. We can use a loop to set this up. Add a **repeat 10** loop and drop the *word length* variable into the number space

8 Inside its bracket, place an **add thing to [list name]** block. Change the text "thing" to a single question mark, and change the list name to *game board*

```
set word length ▼ to  length of  word to guess
repeat  word length
    add  ?  to  game board ▼
```

Beware

Take care with typing the alphabet with the question mark at the end. If you get the letters in the wrong order, you'll see the wrong letters on screen when you play. A small typing error here can spoil the game.

9 There are two other variables we need, one containing the alphabet with a question mark at the end, and the other setting the score to zero. Drag in two **set [variable name] to 0** blocks, and edit them accordingly

```
repeat  word length
    add  ?  to  game board ▼

set  alphabet ▼  to  ABCDEFGHIJKLMNOPQRSTUVWXYZ?
set  score ▼  to  0
```

Showing the game board

Click your alphabet sprite in the Sprite List. As you know, this sprite has 27 costumes, one for each of the letters of the alphabet plus the question mark. Our game board contains an item for each letter in the word the player is guessing. Each item is a letter, if it's been correctly guessed, or a question mark if not.

The heart of this next script is about converting the letters and question marks in the game board into the correct costume number of the sprite, so that it can be stamped on the Stage. Letter C in the game board, for example, needs to be converted into the third costume of the sprite, which shows a letter C:

1 The script is triggered when the message "show board" is received, so start by adding that Event or Control block

2 Add two Looks blocks to hide the sprite and reset the color effect, and a Motion block to position the sprite in the top-left of the Stage

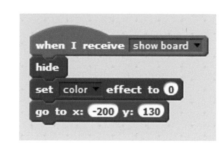

3 The script looks at each letter of the game board in turn. The variable *word marker* is used to remember which letter of the game board we're checking. We start by setting it to zero, because it will be increased by one before we check each letter

4 We need to add a **repeat 10** loop. This loop will be used to check all the spaces in the game board, so replace the number in it with the variable *word length*

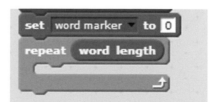

Don't forget

Ransom Writer in Chapter 10 is a more adaptable script for writing on the Stage.

Hot tip

In the outer "repeat block", we could also have used the length of the game board list to say how many times to repeat. There's often more than one right answer in programming.

Beware

Make sure you're adding these scripts to the right sprite (your letter sprite), otherwise the game won't work.

...cont'd

Beware

Scratch sees upper case and lower case letters as being the same. This is quite unusual in programming languages, but makes things much simpler for you. It doesn't matter if you guess an "E" or an "e" when playing the game, as a result.

Don't forget

We're using a loop inside a loop. The outer loop works its way through the game board, one space at a time. It uses the *word marker* variable to remember where it is. The inner loop works its way through the alphabet, one letter at a time. It uses the variable *alphabet marker* to remember where it is.

5 We'll check each character in the *alphabet* variable to see if it matches the game board character. The variable *alphabet marker*

remembers which character in the alphabet we've got to. Start the loop by setting it to zero, and add a block to change *word marker* by 1. This enables us to check the game board characters in order, using the next one each time we repeat the loop

6 Add a **repeat until** block, inside your **repeat** block's bracket. We'll use this to keep checking the game board letter against the alphabet until we find a match. Drag an = Operator into its frame

7 Drag the block **item 1 of [list name]** into your Operator block and choose the list *game board*. Drag in the variable **word marker** block and put it in place of the 1. This identifies the right space in the game board

8 There is an Operator block you can use to refer to a specific letter in a piece of text called **letter 1 of world**. Drag it in to the other side of your Operator block. Replace the text "world" with the variable *alphabet*. Replace the 1 with the variable *alphabet marker*

9 This inner loop repeats until the letter in the game board is the same as the letter in the alphabet. Add a block to increase the variable *alphabet marker*, which counts how far through the alphabet we are

10 When this loop finishes, the variable *alphabet marker* contains the right costume number. That's because the letters and question mark in the variable *alphabet* are in the same order as the costumes. All that remains is to change to that costume, stamp it on the Stage and move the sprite so it's in position for the next letter or question mark. Here's the final script

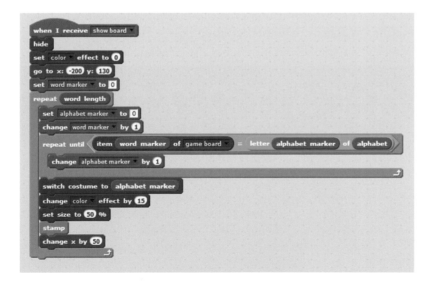

Hot tip

I've used the color effect too to add a tint to the game board letters and question marks.

157

Hot tip

You can stamp a sprite on the Stage even when that sprite is hidden.

Testing the game board

When you're creating programs, it's a good idea to test what you can as you work your way through the program. If you wait until you've finished everything before you test, it's much harder to fix errors. Part of the art of programming is about thinking of ways to test your programs to make sure there are no errors.

Here's a script you can use to test your game board script works as expected. It clears the Stage (to remove any previous game board shown on it), and issues the broadcast "set up variables", which sets up the *game board* and *alphabet* variables for you. This script then replaces the first four letters in the game board with the letters of the word "test". Finally, it issues the broadcast to draw the game board. Click the script to run it.

You should see the word TEST appear on the Stage. If the variable *word to guess* is more than four letters long, you'll see question marks in the other letter spaces.

Don't forget

In the Data or Variables part of the Blocks Palette tick the box beside the variable *word to guess* and the list *game board* to see them on the Stage too.

Asking for the player's guess

Let's add some interaction with the player now!

1 Click the dinosaur, dog or whatever other sprite you're using as your main character in the Sprite List

2 This script is triggered when it receives the message "player inputs letter" so add a hat block to do this. It's an Events or Control block

3 Add a block to switch to the costume dinosaur1-f or dog2-a, or another suitable pose for asking a question

4 We should make sure the player enters just one letter and keep asking them until they do. Add a block to set the variable *letter guessed* to nothing (just delete the 0 in the block), and add a **repeat until** block

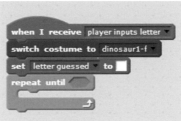

5 We want to repeat until the letter guessed is one letter long, so use the = Operator. Drag the **length of world** Operator block into it and drag the *letter guessed* variable onto that. Change the other side of the = operator to 1

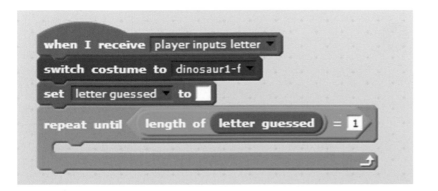

Above: The costume dog2-a. A suitable pose for this part of the game, as the dog wonders which letter you'll guess next.

Hot tip

It's a good idea to make sure the player enters something sensible when we ask them a question. This is called validating the input. In this game, we've checked that they've entered a single character that isn't in the list of previous letters, which should help keep the game on track. If we wanted to go further, we could check that they haven't entered a number or exclamation mark, or something else that isn't a letter.

...cont'd

Beware

When you set the *letter guessed* variable, there's a difference between having nothing in the box, and having a space in there. They look almost the same, but the program won't work if there's a space in there!

Don't forget

Take care with your brackets. The "if" bracket and everything inside it goes inside your "repeat until" bracket, otherwise the player wouldn't be asked to guess again when they guessed the same letter.

Hot tip

Click the green flag to test the game so far. When you enter the same letter twice, the game should tell you.

6 Inside this loop, ask the player to guess a letter. Put their answer into the *letter guessed* variable

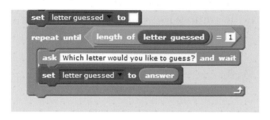

7 Players find it hard to remember which letters they've already guessed, so we should check for them. The list *guessed letters* remembers their previous guesses. Drag an **if** block into your **repeat until** bracket. Drag the **[list name] contains thing** block into the **if** block's frame, click the menu in it to choose the list *guessed letters*, and add the variable *letter guessed* in place of "thing". Inside this **if** bracket, tell the player they've already guessed the letter and set the variable *letter guessed* to be blank again

8 The **repeat until** loop ends when the player has entered a single letter that isn't in the list of previously-guessed letters. To finish this script, we should add their guess to the list of guessed letters for checking on future goes

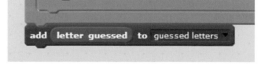

Checking the letter

The next script we should add to our main sprite is the one that checks whether the player's guess is in the word. If it is, it's added to the game board and that's updated on screen. If not, the game adds another stroke to the gallows:

1 Click the dinosaur, dog or whatever other sprite you're using as your main character in the Sprite List

2 This script is triggered when it receives the message "check the letter" so add a hat block to do this. It's an Events or Control block

3 We'll use two variables here. The *was guess right* variable will remember whether the player got any letters right, after we've checked the whole word against their guess. The *letter marker* variable is used to remember our place as we work our way through the word, letter by letter. Start by setting *was guess right* to NO, and *letter marker* to 0

```
when I receive  check the letter ▼
set  was guess right ▼  to  NO
set  letter marker ▼  to  0
```

4 We're going to check each letter in the word against the player's guess, so we need a **repeat 10** block. The number of times we repeat will be the length of the word

```
when I receive  check the letter ▼
set  was guess right ▼  to  NO
set  letter marker ▼  to  0
repeat  word length
```

...cont'd

5 Drag in the **change letter marker by 1** block, so that on each loop we check the next letter in the word

6 Add an **if** block and add the = and **letter 1 of world** Operator blocks. Add the variable blocks as shown to check whether the letter guessed matches the letter in the mystery word that we're checking

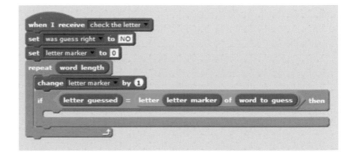

7 The *letter marker* variable also tells us which space in the game board should be changed if the player makes a right guess. Inside the **if** bracket, add a **replace item 1 of [list name] with thing** block, and modify it as shown below to update the game board with the guessed letter. We also need to set the variable *was guess right* to YES, add one to the *score*, and clear the game board and redraw it

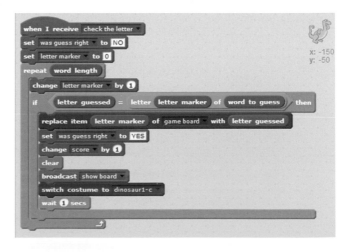

8 When the player guesses right, I've added a switch to a joyful dinosaur costume too, and a 1 second delay so the player has time to see it. You could add a little jump, or some celebratory music

9 When the loop finishes checking for right guesses and updates the game board if there are any, we need to perform two other checks. First, add these blocks to check whether the game has been won, and to change *gameover status* to WON if so. Remember that our main game loop ends when this variable changes. These blocks join to the bottom of the **repeat** block, not inside it

10 The other thing we need to check is whether we need to draw another stroke on the gallows. At the start of the loop, the variable *was guess right* is set to NO. If the player makes a right guess, this is changed to YES. If the loop ends and this variable is still NO, that means the player didn't make a right guess. In that case, we should use the broadcast "wrong guess" to trigger the gallows to draw another stroke. I've also changed the costume to a shocked dinosaur

Game over

The final section we need to write is the game over sequence. This script is triggered when the main game loop ends because the variable *gameover status* has been changed to WON or LOST:

1 Make sure you're still adding scripts to your main sprite. Click it in the Sprite List if necessary

2 This script is triggered when it receives the message "game over" so add a hat block to do this

3 Add an **if... then... else** block. Into the frame of the block, drag the = Operator. Drag the *gameover status* variable into one half of it, and type the word LOST into the other half

4 The first bracket in this block is for what happens when the gameover status is LOST. Drag in three **say Hello! for 2 secs** blocks from the Looks part of the Blocks Palette. Change the messages in the first two to "Oh no! You lost!" and "The word was...". Drag the variable *word to guess* into the third one

5 The other bracket contains blocks that are only used if the gameover status is not LOST, which means the player won. Add a congratulatory message here!

6 Finally, the program should finish here. Click the **Control** button above the Blocks Palette and drag in a **stop all** block. This stops all scripts on all sprites in the program

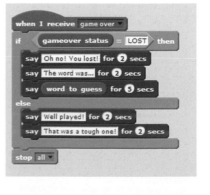

8 Space Swarm

Use what you've learned so far and build on it to make an arcade game. You'll learn how to use loops to create special effects, how to enable a sprite to fire at another sprite, and how to make a high score table.

Introducing Space Swarm

We're under attack! As the aliens swarm around the planet, eager to plunder all of its resources, only one person can save us. You!

Space Swarm, in the spirit of classic arcade games, sees you firing on enemies and dodging their invasion. The aliens rush in towards you from the right of the screen, zig-zagging in random directions. To play the game, move your character with the cursor keys and press the spacebar to fire. You lose one of your three lives each time an alien hits you.

This game brings together much of what you've learned in previous chapters, and will also show you how to:

● Add special effects to make sprites materialize and evaporate

● Enable one sprite to fire upon another

● Use flags to swap information between sprites

● Add looping background music to your game

● Make a high score table that remembers the best score anyone has achieved playing your game on the Scratch website (Scratch 2.0 only)

● Give the player three lives

Beware

Space Swarm runs much faster in Scratch 2.0 than it does in Scratch 1.4 on the Raspberry Pi. The Raspberry Pi team is working on making Scratch faster, though.

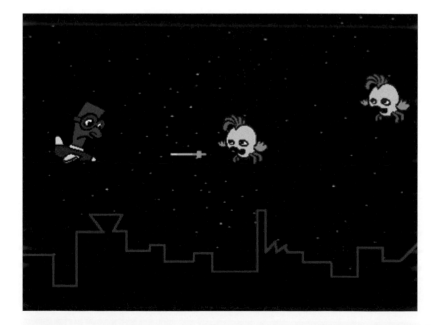

Preparing the images

The first step in building your game is to create some images for your background and sprites:

1 Create your background. Start by importing the stars backdrop (find it in the Space Theme in Scratch 2.0 or Nature Folder in Scratch 1.4). Use the Paint Editor to adapt it. Draw a futuristic skyline at the bottom, and then use the paintbrush with blank ink to blot out the stars below the buildings

2 Add two sprites, one for your player's character and the other for the alien. I picked my sprites from the Fantasy folder of Scratch 1.4 (see bottom of page). The player's character is called fantasy3, and my alien character is called fantasy4. In Scratch 2.0, you could use Robot1 for your player's character and perhaps use the Dragon or Tera sprite for the aliens. Both sprites are in the Fantasy category (see below)

...cont'd

3 Create a sprite to use as your missile. It should be designed as if firing towards the right

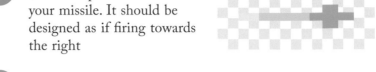

4 Create a sprite to use as your Game Over message. I used a tool to make 3D text and then added the image to Scratch. To use your own image for a sprite, click the folder icon above the Sprite List. It's the third New sprite icon in Scratch 2.0, and the middle one in Scratch 1.4

5 Add a second costume to your alien sprite to show when it is hit by the missile. The alien also gets zapped away into space, so the costume is only shown briefly. I made my costume by duplicating the alien costume and then filling it in in shades of yellow. To duplicate a costume, click the sprite in the Sprite List and click the **Costumes** tab. In Scratch 2.0, right-click on the costume and choose **Duplicate**. In Scratch 1.4, click the **Copy** button beside the costume you want to copy

6 Rename your player's sprite to "ship", your missile sprite to "missile", and your alien to "alien" (see Chapter 4)

Adding sound effects

As you learned in Chapter 5, a sprite can only play sound effects that have been added to it. This game has a techno beat to keep the blood pumping, a scream when the player is hit, a mournful trumpet when the game ends, and some alien noises too:

1 Click the ship sprite in the Sprite List

2 Click the **Sounds** tab, and click the button to choose a sound from the library in Scratch 2.0 (it looks like a small speaker), or the **Import** button in Scratch 1.4

3 Add the sound techno from the Music Loops Category or folder. Repeat these steps to add the sound scream-male1 from the Human Category or folder

4 Click the alien in the Sprite List and add the spiral sound effect. It is in the Electronic Category or folder

5 Add the laser1 sound to your missile sprite. It's also among the Electronic sound effects

6 The sprite with the Game Over message needs three sounds: trumpet1, trumpet2 and triumph (to be played when there's a new high score, so only required in Scratch 2.0). The trumpet sounds are in the Instruments Category or folder, and triumph is among the Music Loops

Don't forget

Refer back to Chapter 5 for detailed advice on adding sound effects to a sprite if you need help.

Creating the variables

In this game, we're going to use cloud variables for the first time. They enable information from your project to be saved centrally on the Scratch computers, and then accessed by other people who use your project. Space Swarm uses the cloud variable *high score* to remember the highest score that anyone has ever achieved in the game.

You create cloud variables in the same way you make ordinary variables, by clicking the **Data** button, and then clicking the **Make a Variable** button in the Blocks Palette. Enter your variable name, tick the box beside "Cloud variable", and click **OK**. Cloud variables are always available for all sprites. After you've made one, you can identify it because it has a fluffy cloud symbol in its block (see above).

We'll use three variables in this program:

- *score*: This variable will keep track of the score in the current game. In this game, the player and alien sprites will use it, so create it for all sprites.

- *player hit*: We'll use this variable to remember whether the player has been hit or not, by storing the words "YES" or "NO" in it. When there are lots of scripts working at the same time, a variable like this can be used to keep track of the state of the game. In this game, we'll use this variable to stop the player from moving or firing after they've been hit. Create this variable and make it work for all sprites. Variables that are used like this to remember the state of part of the game are sometimes called flags.

- *high score*: Create this variable and tick the box to make it a cloud variable. Cloud variables are only available in Scratch 2.0, so ignore this variable if you're using Scratch 1.4.

Programming the hero

Now the variables have been set up, we can start to build the scripts for our hero character, which the player will control:

1 Click your ship sprite in the Sprite List. Drag in a Data or Variable block to reset *score* to zero. The player and aliens can use the full Stage area, so hide the *score* and *high score* variables to stop them getting in the way

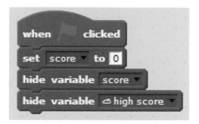

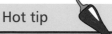

Hot tip

You can make the game easier by making the player's character smaller, so the aliens are less likely to hit it. Lower the value in the block that sets its size.

2 We're going to assemble blocks next that make the player appear, give the player control until they die, and then show what happens when they're hit. To give the player three lives, we'll do all of this three times. Drag a **repeat 10** Control block into your script, and change the number to 3

3 The variable *player hit* is used to remember whether the player has been hit or not. At the start of each life, we set it to NO

4 Add the blocks to set up the sprite's appearance, including moving it to the front (so it appears on top of all other sprites), clearing graphic effects, and putting it in its starting position (x:-165, y:0) and direction (90, facing right). For my sprite, I set the size to 50%. If you're using a different sprite, you might need to use a different size

...cont'd

Below: The last half of the teleport sequence. This happens rapidly, so players will just see blobs of color coming together to make the ship appear in space.

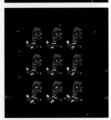

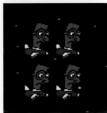

5 We'll make the sprite teleport in by using the mosaic effect. Starting it high and reducing it to zero makes the sprite materialize as if it's arrived in pieces and then morphed together

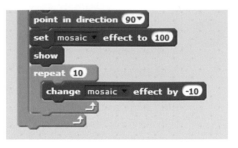

6 Add a **repeat until** Control block. Add the = Operator block into its frame. Drag the *player hit* variable into one side, and type YES into the other side. We'll use this loop to enable the player to move until they're hit

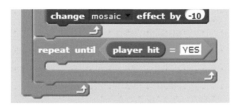

7 Add the blocks to control the sprite inside the bracket of the **repeat until** block. These are similar to the controls you used for Dodgeball

8 In that script, the direction is adjusted to point the ship in the direction it travels, purely for presentation. The numbers used for the tilt in direction aren't evenly spaced. I subtract 20 from 90 to point up, but only add 10 to 90 to point down. I tried 110, but this sprite design already tilts down slightly, so the effect looks better using 100

Don't forget

Broadcast blocks are Event blocks in Scratch 2.0 and Control blocks in Scratch 1.4. Click the menu in the block to make a new broadcast.

9 When the **repeat until** loop ends, the player has died. The sequence for losing a life makes the ship spin in a circle and fade away using the ghost effect. The scream-male1 sound gives an audible yelp. Put these blocks outside the **repeat until** bracket, but inside your **repeat 3** bracket

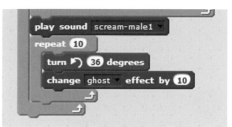

10 Finally, hide the sprite and add a short delay before the next life begins. Send a broadcast "cloak alien", which hides the aliens so they can't hit the player while the ship is materializing. These blocks go inside your **repeat 3** bracket, but outside any other brackets

11 When the **repeat 3** loop ends, the player has died three times, so it's game over. Create a broadcast called "game over" to alert all the other sprites. This block joins underneath your **repeat 3**

173

Enabling the player to fire

To enable the player to fire, we'll add a script to the player's sprite that broadcasts "fire" when the player presses the space bar, and we'll tell our missile sprite to move when it receives that broadcast:

1 Click the ship in the Sprite List

2 Add a script to the sprite that continuously checks for the spacebar being pressed, and then broadcasts "fire" and waits when it is

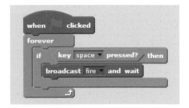

3 Click the missile sprite in the Sprite List

4 Add this script to your sprite, to hide the missile when the game starts, and position it behind the ship

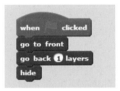

5 Add a script for when the broadcast "fire" is received. We don't want to fire when the player has been hit, so we wrap everything in an **if** block that checks for this. The script moves the sprite to the ship's position, and then lowers it slightly, so the missile comes from the ship and not the pilot's head. The loop moves the missile right until it's off screen

6 Click that last script to see the missile fire

Moving and shooting aliens

The alien uses the pixelate effect to materialize in a random position on the right. It makes a zig-zag pattern across the Stage by pointing in a random left-facing direction, making eight movements, and then changing direction,

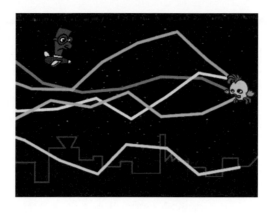

until it reaches the left of the Stage. The picture shows paths in different colors, drawn with the pen:

Don't forget

You can have several scripts on the same sprite, and you can use the green flag to start any of them.

1 Click the alien in the Sprite List. Add the **when green flag clicked** block and a block to set the size of your sprite. Mine is 50%

2 Fix the rotation style to left-right, using the **set rotation style left-right** block in Scratch 2.0. In Scratch 1.4, use the settings above the Blocks Palette instead (see Chapter 2)

3 Add a **forever** block. The alien is always moving. When it's dead, it's hidden, but still keeps moving

4 Inside your **forever** bracket add the blocks that put your sprite in a random position on the right of the screen and use the pixelate effect to make it appear

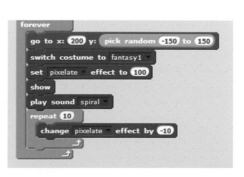

Hot tip

If you've used a different alien sprite to me, adjust the size of the sprite in this script as appropriate. Smaller aliens make it easier for the player to avoid hitting them, but make it harder for the missile to hit them too.

...cont'd

Above: Arrows indicate the range of directions the sprite can choose. The upper arrow shows direction -45, and the lower one shows -135. The alien can randomly pick any direction between them to move left across the Stage.

Beware

We use the variable to store whether the player's been hit, instead of using a broadcast to tell the other sprites, because a broadcast is used to start a new script running. Instead, we need to change how the existing scripts behave, especially the ship script that gives us three lives.

5 Add the movement script. It repeats until the sprite is off the Stage, pointing in a random direction and then moving 8 times. During our **repeat 8** loop, we need to check if the sprite goes off Stage and hide it if so because the random direction means we don't know when the alien will reach the edge. This script goes inside your **forever** bracket

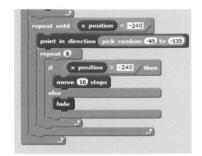

6 Add this separate script to hide the sprite while the player is materializing. The alien continues to cross the screen unseen and re-appears when it rematerializes at the right

7 The final alien script detects when it touches the ship or missile. When the player is hit, the variable *player hit* is set to YES. When the alien touches the missile (which means the alien's been shot), the costume changes to the 'hit' costume, the *score* increases, and a loop reduces the sprite's size to 0. It looks like the alien drifts away in space. The sprite is hidden and its size reset, and it is moved off the left of the screen. That makes the movement loop in the other alien script end, so the alien regenerates again on the right

Finishing touches

Now add the final touches to your game!

1 Add this script to your ship sprite to play music throughout the game. The **if** block stops the tune from starting again during the Game Over sequence

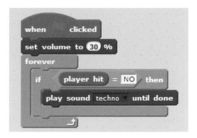

2 Duplicate the alien sprite. Now you have two aliens to contend with!

3 Click the Game Over sprite and add a script to hide the message when the game begins

4 Add this script to play the trumpet, zoom the sprite in by increasing its size, play the second trumpet and then show the variable *score*

177

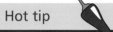

5 Finally, use the **stop all** block to stop all scripts on all sprites

Hot tip

Try customizing the game. You could give each alien a different movement pattern and design, or make one faster than the other (change the number of steps it moves).

Above: The final Game Over screen, with one alien still shown.

Adding the high score

One way to keep players coming back for more is to challenge them to be the best ever at the game. In Space Swarm, we'll keep a record of the highest score achieved (by any players playing the game on the Scratch website), and play a triumphant tune if the player beats the record. This feature only works in Scratch 2.0.

Add this script immediately before the **stop all** block in your game over script:

1 The best ever score is stored in the cloud variable *high score*. Drag in **show variable high score**

2 Drag in an **if** Control block. We're going to see whether one number is higher than another, so drag the > Operator block into its frame

3 Drag the *score* variable into the left of the > block, and the *high score* variable into the right of it

4 Inside the **if** bracket, put the blocks we want to run if this is a new high score. A block here updates *high score* to the player's *score*, and then plays some triumphant music to celebrate!

In Scratch 2.0, there is a "username" Sensing block. This tells you the player's username on the Scratch website. You can use it to greet or congratulate players who use your games with a script like the one below.

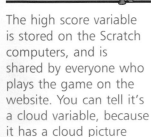

Don't forget

The high score variable is stored on the Scratch computers, and is shared by everyone who plays the game on the website. You can tell it's a cloud variable, because it has a cloud picture beside its name in the variable blocks.

9

Scratch hardware projects

Use Scratch to interact with your webcam and microphone, detect sensors on a PicoBoard and switch on a light connected to the Raspberry Pi.

Don't forget

The webcam is supported only in Scratch 2.0, but the "loudness" block works in Scratch 1.4 if you have a microphone.

Hot tip

You can use the tickboxes beside the "loudness" and "video motion on this sprite" blocks to see their values on the Stage. This can help you with testing your programs.

Using a webcam

Scratch 2.0 enables you to use a webcam to interact with your programs. These are the Sensing blocks you use for this:

- **turn video on**: Before you can start using the webcam, you have to turn the video on. The video looks like a mirror, so writing is reversed. There's an option in this block to turn the video on flipped, which fixes that. There's also an option to turn video off when you no longer need it.

- **set video transparency to 50%**: The video appears on top of the Stage, and you can decide how much of the background you want to show through. Change the percentage to 0 to see only the video with no background, and change it to 100 to see just the background, without any video. When using video to control a sprite, the user will need to see themselves on screen, so 50 is often ideal.

- **video motion on this sprite**: This block measures how much the video image is moving under the sprite. You can use the menu in it to detect video direction instead of motion, and to detect video on the entire Stage instead of a sprite. It gives a percentage number, so you can adjust the sensitivity by requiring a lower number (to make the program more sensitive) or a higher number (to make it less sensitive to movement).

- **loudness**: You can use this block to detect how loud the sound is that the webcam is receiving. It's also a percentage, so requiring a lower number makes your program more sensitive to sound.

Responding to warnings

When you use the webcam with Scratch, you'll receive a warning. This is to protect your privacy and stop programs and websites from using the webcam without your permission. When you see the Adobe warning, click the **Allow** button (see left).

Using video direction

Here's a simple demonstration that shows how you can use the video direction on a sprite to control it. The Sensing blocks are new to you, but the rest of the program should hold no surprises if you've read the earlier chapters.

After turning the video on and setting it to fill the screen with no background showing through (0% transparency), we put the sprite in the middle of the screen. We then start a **forever** loop. This checks whether there is video motion on the sprite, and uses a fairly high sensitivity for this. If there is, it points the sprite in the direction of the motion and moves it 20 steps.

When you run the program, you can nudge the sprite around the screen using your hand. I've used a beetle sprite because that looks quite natural crawling over the screen in all directions.

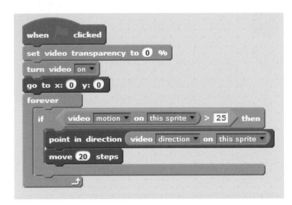

To make more of a game of it, add the donut sprite from the Sprite Library and give it the script below. Now the goal is to steer the beetle to the donut, which will then disappear and reappear in a random position.

Hot tip

Visit my website to find a variation on this script which enables you to paint in rainbow colors on the Stage by moving your hands.

Hot tip

Face the flat or back of your hand to the camera. It makes it easier for the camera to detect your hand movements, and makes the program work better as a result.

Hot tip

I used 20 steps in the beetle's movement here because the sprite needs to be able to move at the same speed as my hand, and this felt right. Experiment to see what works well for you, depending on your webcam setup and how fast you move your hand.

Going Batty

There's nothing like a nice peaceful walk in the castle grounds, but with all these bats flying around, it's hard to enjoy it. Wave your hands to shoo them away. You'll have to keep at it, though, because they keep coming back!

Going Batty demonstrates video motion on a sprite. It also provides another example of sprite cloning, which you learned about in Chapter 4:

1 Add the backdrop that shows the path leading up to the castle. It's one of several images in the Castle Theme

2 Add the sprite Bat2. It has two costumes that make the bat flap its wings when you switch between them

Below: Here I am trying to shoo away the bats!

Don't forget

The blocks related to cloning are all Control blocks. Click the Control button above the Blocks Palette to find them. Remember, they're only available in Scratch 2.0.

3 Add the following script to the bat to turn the video on and set the transparency so the castle and player can both be seen. The bat also hides itself because this sprite doesn't move: its clones do.

The script then enters a **forever** loop that makes clones of the bat, with a quarter of a second between each one. At a rate of four bats per second, it won't be long before the air is thick with them!

```
when [flag] clicked
hide
turn video on ▾
set video transparency to 65 %
forever
    create clone of myself ▾
    wait 0.25 secs
```

4 Add the script below to the bat. When each clone is created, it is pointed in a random direction, set to a random size (between 50% and 100%), and shown on the Stage. The motion works in a similar way to the beachballs you used in Chapter 4: the bats keep moving forwards, and use the **if on edge bounce** block to change direction when they reach the edge of the Stage. The loop also continuously checks for video motion on the sprite. If it's above 90%, the clone is deleted. If not, the loop keeps moving the sprite and checking for movement

```
when I start as a clone
show
point in direction  pick random -179 to 180
set size to  pick random 50 to 100 %
forever
    move 10 steps
    if on edge, bounce
    if  video motion ▾ on this sprite ▾  > 90  then
        delete this clone
```

5 Finally, add this script to the bat sprite to make it flap its wings

```
when I start as a clone
forever
    next costume
    wait 0.5 secs
```

Using a PicoBoard

The PicoBoard enables you to take your Scratch programming skills into the real world, by interacting with various sensors that are built in to it, or that you connect to it. It plugs into your computer using a USB cable and includes the following:

Hot tip

At the time of writing, the PicoBoard only works with Scratch 1.4. In the future, compatibility with the downloadable version of Scratch 2.0 might be added.

- **slider**: Scratch can detect the position of the slider, and give you a number from 0 to 100 to represent it. You can use the slider for controlling the position of sprites on screen or the volume, for example.

- **light sensor**: This detects how much light is falling on it, and gives you a percentage. On the PicoBoard, the sensor is in the middle of an eye picture.

- **sound sensor**: This sensor is used to detect how much noise there is. On the Pico Board, it's a round component with a picture of an ear next to it.

- **button**: This is a push button you can detect being pressed.

- **A, B, C, D**: There are four sockets on the Pico Board that you can attach cables to. The cables included end in crocodile clips (also known as alligator clips). You can connect these to your own circuits, and then measure the amount of resistance in them. When you touch the clips to each other, there is no resistance and the value is 0. When they are completely disconnected, no current can flow between them, so there is the maximum resistance of 100. You can use these sockets to detect switches, so you can make your own game controllers.

184

Hot tip

Resistance just means how much opposition there is to electrical current. A wire has low resistance, because electricity passes through it easily. A brick has high resistance, because it doesn't conduct electricity.

Right: The PicoBoard, with the slider at the top, and the sockets on the left.

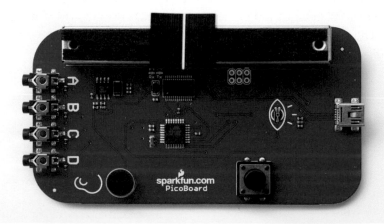

Making a clap-o-meter

There are two Sensing blocks that are used to interact with the PicoBoard. Both blocks have a menu in them so you can choose one of the sensors on the PicoBoard to use with the block. The blocks are:

- **slider sensor value**: This block gives you a number between 0 and 100. You can click the menu in it to change the slider sensor to the light or sound sensor, or to one of the A, B, C, and D sockets.

- **sensor button pressed?**:
This block tells you if the button is pressed, or if the A, B, C or D circuit is connected. If you connect a switch to the A socket, for example, the circuit will be connected when the switch is pressed.

You can use the **sensor value** block in place of a number in your script. Here's a simple script, for example, that creates a clap-o-meter. To try it, just add it to your cat Sprite1. The more noise you make, the higher your sprite will climb up the screen. It works by turning the value of the sound sensor (which will be between 1 and 100) into the sprite's y position.

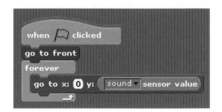

If you want to keep a record of the highest position reached, add this script to another sprite. There's a Sensing block that can detect the x or y position of another sprite, so we use that here to check the y position of Sprite1. If Sprite1 is higher, this sprite goes to its position. As a result, this sprite will always be at the highest point the clap-o-meter sprite has reached.

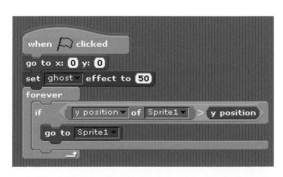

185

Beware

The "sound sensor" and the "loudness" blocks do much the same job, but they aren't the same thing. To sense sound using the Picoboard, use the "sound sensor" block. For your microphone, use the "loudness" block.

Beware

The "sensor value" block also includes options for tilt and distance, but these aren't supported in the PicoBoard.

Making Night Flight

You can use the PicoBoard to make a game controller too. In this simple demonstration, you control a witch as she goes about her nightly flight, using the slider to move left and right, and the push button to go up. As night falls, the woods get dark, too.

1 Start a new project and add the woods background. It's in the Nature folder. Add the witch1 sprite from the Fantasy folder. Delete the cat

2 Click the Stage beside the Sprite List and click the **Scripts** tab if necessary

3 Drag in a **when green flag clicked** block and a **forever** block. They're both Control blocks

4 Drag a **set color effect to 0** block into the bracket of your **forever** block. Change the effect to brightness

5 We're going to use the light sensor to decide how bright the background should be. If we use the light sensor value to set the brightness without adjusting it, the background will go from normal to extremely bright, which looks odd. We want the brightness to start at -75, so the numbers go from -75 to 25 (night to dusk) instead of from 0 to 100. Drag the + Operator block into your brightness block

6 Type -75 into one of the holes in your Operator block. Click the **Sensing** button above the Blocks Palette and drag the **slider sensor value** block into the other half. Change the sensor in it to be the **light** sensor

7 Click your witch sprite in the Sprite List. Drag in a **when green flag clicked** block, and a Motion block **set y to 0**. Change the number in it to -70, so the witch starts fairly low down the Stage. Drag in a **forever** block and put an **if** block inside its bracket. Click the **Sensing** button above the Blocks Palette and drag the **sensor button pressed?** block into the frame of your **if** block. Inside the bracket of the block, add a **change y by 10** block. This makes the witch move up the screen 10 steps when the PicoBoard button is pressed

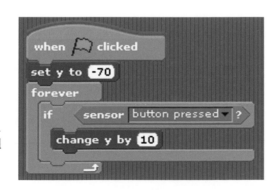

Hot tip

This example shows you how to move a sprite with the PicoBoard. You could add your own goals and enemies to turn this into a game.

...cont'd

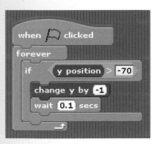

8 Drag a **set x to 0** Motion block into your script. Put it inside your **forever** bracket, but outside your **if** bracket

9 The slider gives a number from 0 to 100, but we'd like to use it to move a sprite across almost the whole width of the Stage. We need to convert the slider's number into one that goes from -200 to 200. To do that, we multiply the slider number by 4 (giving us a number between 0 and 400), and then subtract 200. Drag the - Operator block into your **set x to 0** block. Type 200 into the right of it

10 Drag a * Operator block (for multiplication) into the left of your - Operator

11 Drag the **slider sensor value** block into one side of the * block and type the number 4 into the other side. This will move the witch's x position to a value between -200 and 200 depending on the slider value

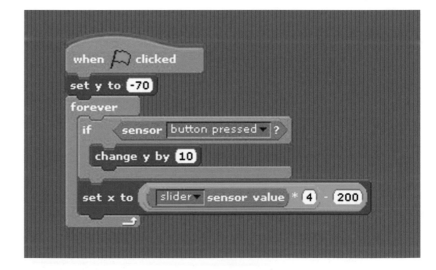

Using the Raspberry Pi GPIO

The Raspberry Pi has a series of pins in the top-left corner of the board, on its top surface, called General Purpose Input/Output pins (GPIO pins). These pins can be used to connect your own electronics projects to the Raspberry Pi, which you can then control using software. You can use an extension to Scratch to interact with the GPIO pins:

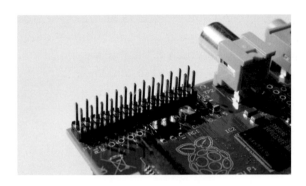

Beware

Don't connect things to the GPIO pins unless you know what you're doing. You could break your Raspberry Pi. Neither the author nor publisher can take responsibility if you break your Raspberry Pi!

1 For this project, you will need a light emitting diode (LED), and a resistor of at least 330 ohm. If you don't have a single resistor of that value, you can join two lower-value resistors together end to end to add up to at least 330 ohm

Hot tip

Pi-Cars makes and sells kits for steering remote-controlled cars from Scratch on the Raspberry Pi. See **www.pi-cars.com**

2 An LED has a long leg and a short leg. At the base of the LED's dome, it is flat above the short leg, so you can tell them apart even after you've separated them

3 Gently bend the LED's legs apart and connect your resistor to the long leg of your LED. If you don't know how to solder, you can do this by just twisting the resistor's wire around the LED's leg

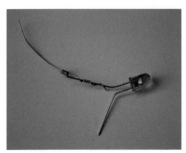

Hot tip

An LED is a component that lights up and that only allows electrical current to pass through it in one direction. A resistor is a component that limits the amount of current going through a circuit. In this project, it's here to protect the Raspberry Pi.

...cont'd

Hot tip

You could use your LED to transmit Morse code, or to make a reaction tester, turning the light on and then timing how long it takes the player to tap the spacebar.

Hot tip

It's okay to connect your LED and resistor while the Raspberry Pi is switched on, but usually you should switch off your Raspberry Pi before connecting something to the GPIO pins.

Hot tip

To find out more about how you can use ScratchGPIO, visit Simon Walters' blog at http://cymplecy.wordpress.com
He created ScratchGPIO and has written instructions for it across four blog posts.

4 Connect a female-to-female jumper wire to one leg of the LED and another to the other end of your resistor

5 Position your Raspberry Pi so the logo on the top is the right way up. The bottom row of pins is odd, starting at 1 on the left and going up to 25 on the right. The top row of pins is even, starting at 2 and going up to 26. Using the jumper wire, connect the resistor end of your LED to pin 11 and the other end to pin 25

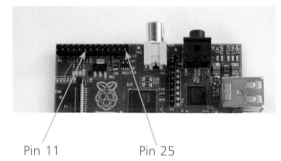

Pin 11   Pin 25

6 To install the software you need on your Raspberry Pi, type this in at the command prompt (double-click on LXTerminal if you're in the graphical interface): **sudo wget https://dl.dropbox.com/s/oql4qzm8jlnsbeb/ install_scratch_gpio2.sh -O /boot/install_scratch_ gpio2.sh**. Note that the character after the hyphen is a capital O, not a number

7 Enter this command at the prompt: **sudo /boot/install_ scratch_gpio2.sh**

8 Enter **startx** to go into the desktop environment. Double-click your new ScratchGPIO icon on the desktop

9 Click the File menu and open the example blink11. When it runs, your LED should flash on and off. It does this by broadcasting the message "pin11high" and "pin11low"

10 Seven shorties

To finish up, here are seven short programs you can build and experiment with. You'll also learn how to make your own blocks in Scratch 2.0.

Keepy-Uppy

In this game, a cross between football and Pong, you have to keep the ball in play. Each time it hits the wall, it knocks a chunk out. The aim is to get it through the other side of the wall:

1 Add the sprite girl3 (in Scratch 2.0) or girl3-running (in Scratch 1.4), plus the sprite Soccer Ball (in Scratch 2.0) or soccer1 in Scratch 1.4. Delete the cat sprite

2 Click the girl sprite in the Sprite List and add this script to position it and enable it to move left and right

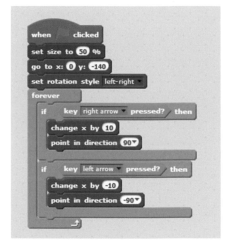

3 Paint a new backdrop, choose green in the color palette and use the fill tool to fill the whole Stage. Add a red box that spans the full width of the Stage, but leave room at the top for the ball to get out

Beware

Scratch 1.4 doesn't have the block to set the rotation style. Instead, click the sprite's button to fix the rotation to left-right. You can find it above the Scripts Area. It's the middle button.

...cont'd

④ Click the ball, and add this script to it

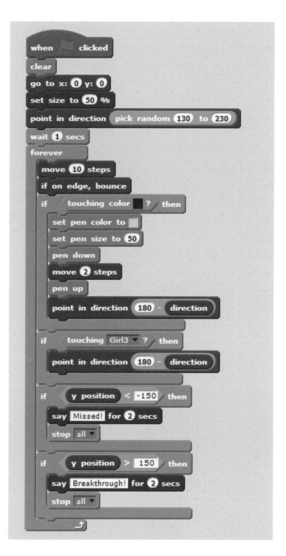

```
when [flag] clicked
clear
go to x: 0 y: 0
set size to 50 %
point in direction (pick random 130 to 230)
wait 1 secs
forever
    move 10 steps
    if on edge, bounce
    if < touching color [ ] ? > then
        set pen color to [ ]
        set pen size to 50
        pen down
        move 2 steps
        pen up
        point in direction (180 - direction)

    if < touching Girl3 ? > then
        point in direction (180 - direction)

    if < y position < -150 > then
        say Missed! for 2 secs
        stop all

    if < y position > 150 > then
        say Breakthrough! for 2 secs
        stop all
```

Hot tip

When you're setting the colors in the "touching color?" and "set pen color" blocks, use the color picker to choose them from your backdrop on the Stage.

Don't forget

Change "touching Girl3" to use whatever your player sprite is called.

Beware

It looks like the wall is breaking down, but actually you're drawing on top of it in the same color as the background. This game won't work with a patterned background, as a result.

⑤ To improve this game, you could add a score that increases each time the ball bounces off the girl, and add some randomness in the direction the ball goes after touching the player. You could improve presentation with a title screen, sound effects, and proper winning and losing sequences. If you have a PicoBoard, you could add slider control, too

Shop Cat

Can you help the Scratch cat to cross the road safely to do its shopping, and then take it home again? This game includes multiple obstacles and a script you can use to control the cat using the keyboard in any game:

1 Add the background of the night city with a street. It's in the Outdoors Category or folder

2 Rename your cat sprite to Cat

3 Add one of the vehicle sprites. They're in the Transportation Category or folder. I used Car-Bug

4 Add this script (right) to your vehicle

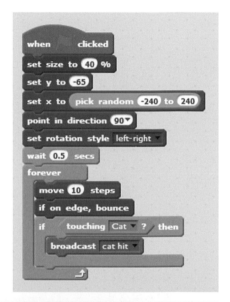

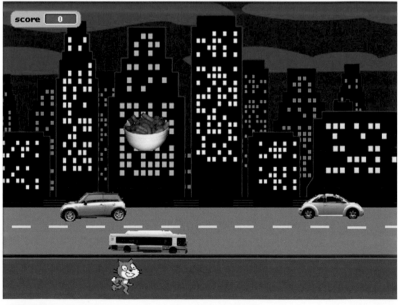

5 Right-click your vehicle sprite in the Sprite List and choose **Duplicate** twice, to create two more vehicles

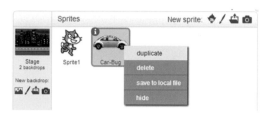

Hot tip

You can reuse the main cat script here in any games that require movement. It enables the cat to move up, down, left and right under keyboard control.

6 Click one of the vehicle sprites, and change the number -65 in the **set y to -65** block to -108. This puts that vehicle on the lower lane of the road. Change the speed of the duplicate vehicles too by editing the number of steps moved in the script from 10 to 15 and 12

7 You can add other costumes to the duplicate vehicles, so it doesn't look like everyone's going to a VW Beetle convention! See Chapter 5 for advice on adding costumes

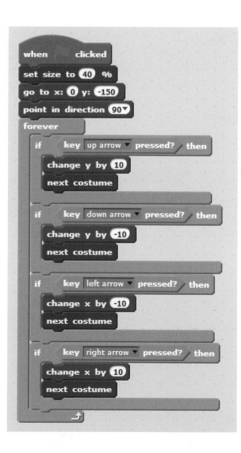

8 Click the cat and add this script (see right) to it. In Scratch 1.4, add the costume cat1-b to see the cat's legs move as it walks

Hot tip

This game shows how you can detect the y position of a sprite from a different sprite. Use the Sensing block "x position of [sprite name]", and click the menu to change it to the y position. This block also detects a sprite's direction, costume, size and volume.

195

...cont'd

9 Add this script to the cat. When a vehicle hits the cat, it broadcasts the message "cat hit". This script then knocks the cat on its back and stops the game

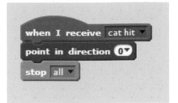

10 Add a new sprite to represent the shopping. Add additional costumes for other shopping items. I added the bananas, fruit salad and cheesy puffs. In Scratch 2.0, there's also an apple and donut

11 Click the **Data** or **Variables** button above the Blocks Palette and make a variable called *score* for all sprites

12 Add the following script to your shopping item sprite. When the cat touches the shopping, the shopping hides and waits until the cat reaches the bottom of the screen again before showing the next item

Above: The costumes used on the sprite to represent the shopping in Scratch 2.0.

Penguin Patter

In Penguin Patter, you can chat to a friendly penguin about life, the universe and everything. As you chat away, he learns what you say and starts using your own phrases to chat back to you:

1. Add your choice of background and sprite. I've used the sprite Penguin2 Talk and malibu beach backdrop. Delete the cat

What shall we talk about?

Let's talk about the weather

197

2. Click the **Data** or **Variables** button above the Blocks Palette. Make the variable *random choice* and the list *sayings*. There's only one sprite in this project, so it doesn't matter whether they're shared or not. Untick the boxes in the Blocks Palette to hide them

3. Add this script to your sprite

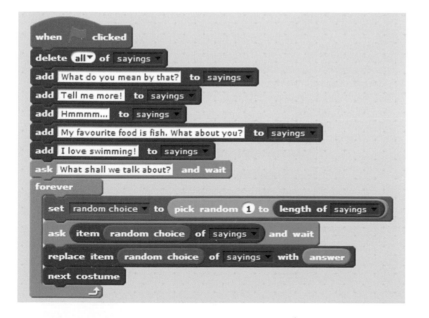

Beware

If you're using Scratch 1.4, there isn't a penguin sprite, but the lion1-a sprite works well for this, together with the woods background.

Hot tip

I used a variable to remember which saying was randomly chosen, so the program can replace it with what the player enters.

Hot tip

Customize this game with your own personality. You can add lots more sayings at the start, and the program works better the more you add.

Ransom Writer

In Chapter 7, you saw how to write on the Stage, but the script was embedded in Hangman. Here's a script that's easier to reuse. I've customized it with letters that look like they've been clipped from a newspaper, like a ransom letter in an old police drama:

1 Click the **Data** or **Variables** button above the Blocks Palette and set up the variables shown right for all sprites

alphabet

alphabetmarker

text-x

text-y

word-to-write

wordmarker

2 The writing script goes onto a sprite with 27 costumes (for the letters A to Z, plus an empty costume). Create this sprite now. See Chapter 7 for advice on making this sprite. I've made my letters using Microsoft Paint

3 Add the script below to your sprite

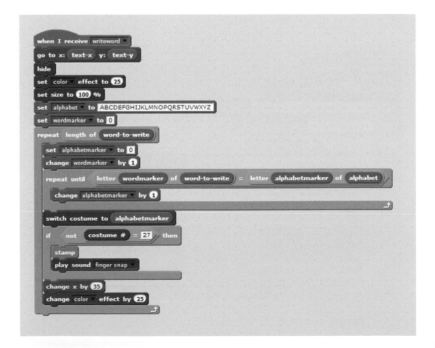

4 To use the script, set the variable *text-x* to be the x coordinate of where you want the text to appear, *text-y* to be the y coordinate and *word-to-write* to be the text. Then broadcast the message "writeword" to trigger the alphabet sprite to write

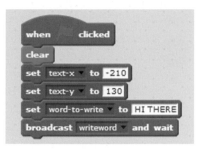

Making your own blocks in Scratch 2.0

Ransom Writer works in both Scratch 2.0 and Scratch 1.4, but in Scratch 2.0, it's possible to make your own blocks. That means you don't have to use variables to carry information to a script like this. It can also make your programs easier to read. The drawback is that you can only use a block you've made from the same sprite you made it on:

1 Click your text-writing sprite in the Sprite List

2 Click the **More Blocks** button above the Blocks Palette and click the **Make a Block** button

3 A window opens with a purple block in it. Type the name of your new block into this block

4 Click the **Options** menu under the purple block to open it. Click **Add label text**, and type 'x:' into the box. Click **Add number input**. Repeat this Step, but this time type 'y:' into the box

5 Click **Add label text**, and type 'text:' into the box. Click **Add string input**

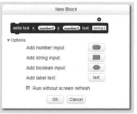

199

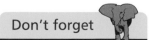

...cont'd

Hot tip

You can download the font I've used in this project from my website at www.sean.co.uk

6 Click the **OK** button

7 Your script now has a **define** block. Join your writer script underneath this to run it when your new block is used. You can drag the blue *number1*, *number2* and *string1* blocks from the **define** block into your script. I've dragged **number1** and **number2** blocks into the **go to x:0 y:0** block (see right)

8 To finish the Ransom Writer script, replace the variable *word-to-write* in it with the **string1** block

9 You can add your new block to your scripts by dragging it in from the **More Blocks** part of the Blocks Palette (right)

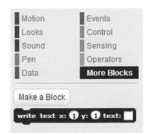

Beware

When you make your own block, you can only use it on the same sprite you defined it on.

10 You can now use your block like you would any other!

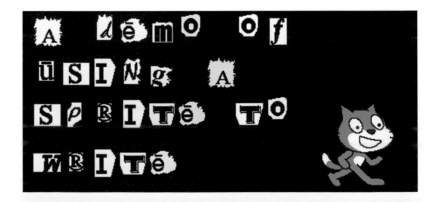

Maze Mania

This simple script enables you to play a maze, and keeps you honest by stopping you from walking through the walls. You can draw your maze as a Stage backdrop or a sprite costume. I created mine using Maze Generator (**www.mazegenerator.net**), with dimensions of 30 by 20, and then imported that as a sprite costume. All your walls need to be the same color. To stop your sprite snagging on walls, use a round sprite:

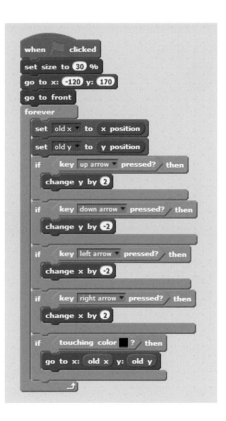

1 Add the script to the sprite that will move through the maze

2 Set your sprite's starting position and adjust the size of your sprite in the script to make it fit comfortably between the walls. Use the color picker to choose the color of the walls in the **touching colour?** block

Hot tip

If you're drawing your own maze, use the line drawing tools to keep your lines straight.

Don't forget

You must make the *old x* and *old y* variables before you can use them in your scripts.

Hot tip

You can enhance this program by adding a target sprite and detecting when it's touched, or adding multiple levels.

Abstract Artist

Unleash the creative genius in your computer with Abstract Artist, a program that makes a random, continuously changing artwork:

1 Start a new project and add this script below to your cat sprite. It makes the cat glide to random points on the screen, while hidden

```
when     clicked
hide
forever
    glide 5 secs to x: pick random -240 to 240 y: pick random -180 to 180
```

2 Right-click the cat sprite in the Sprite List and click **Duplicate**. Now there are two invisible, prowling cats

```
when     clicked
hide
clear
set pen size to 4
pen up
forever
    go to Sprite1
    pen down
    change pen color by 2
    go to Sprite2
    change pen shade by 2
```

3 Add a new sprite (it doesn't matter which) and give it the script shown right. The script makes it flit between the two invisible cats, drawing a line in a new color each time

4 Paint a new background, and fill it with a solid dark color, to make the brightly-colored art really pop out

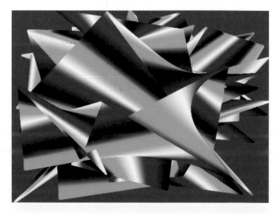

Photo Safari

Go on safari in this game and see if you are quick enough to be a wildlife photographer. The animals appear at random times, and you have to be quick to click them if you want to get that shot!

Hot tip

This game uses a "repeat until" block to wait for 10 seconds before ending the game (see next page). In Scratch 2.0, there's also a hat block you can use to start scripts after a certain time. It's an Events block called "when loudness > 10", and it has a menu so you can start scripts instead when the timer or video motion reach a certain level.

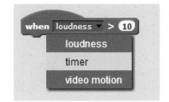

1. Delete the cat sprite. You won't need it in this game

2. Add the water and rocks background from the Nature Category or folder

3. Add the bat1 or bat1-a sprite from the Animals Category or folder (right)

4. Click the **Data** or **Variables** button and make a variable called *score*

5. Add this simple script to the bat sprite. It hides the bat (ready for the game start), puts it in the top left and shrinks it to 75%. During the game, the script makes the bat continuously appear and disappear at random intervals of between 1 and 4 seconds

6. Add this script to the bat to increase the score and hide the sprite when it is clicked

7. Import five additional animal sprites and copy the scripts from your bat sprite to them. To copy a script, click the bat sprite in the Sprite List, and drag the script from its Scripts Area over another sprite in the Sprite List. When you release the mouse button, your script is copied across to that sprite

Beware

In Scratch 1.4, "when this sprite clicked" is a Control block called "when Sprite1 clicked".

...cont'd

8 Go into each sprite and adjust the x and y position in the script, so the animals are spread around the screen. I put a frog on a rock at x:162 y:-125; a ladybug at x:25 y:-65; the butterfly at x:-155 y:-130; a parrot at x:130 y:85; and a monkey at x:-50 y:75

9 Change the random numbers used in the script of each sprite depending on how often you want it to appear. The **wait** block *after* the **show** block determines how long it's shown for. The other **wait** block decides how long it's hidden for

10 Create a new sprite that says Game Over. I made mine in Word so I could use a funky font. I pressed the Print Screen key, pasted into Paint, and then saved the image

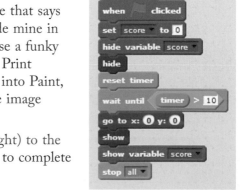

11 Add this script (right) to the Game Over sprite to complete the game

Above: The Stage when the game ends.

11 Making and sharing projects

Now it's time to make your own projects! Discover tips and resources to help here.

Making your own programs

Now you've seen how programs are built in Scratch, you can start to design and share your own creations. Here are some tips:

1 It's rare to program something that works first time unless it's a really simple program. Programming is all about trying something out, testing it, and then changing your scripts. Keep testing your program as you build it. You can click a script in the Scripts Area to run it straight away without running your whole program.

2 If you need to reset the position or look of a sprite for testing, remember you can click blocks in the Blocks Palette to use them on your sprite straight away.

3 If you're having problems with a variable, click the tickbox beside it in the Data or Variables part of the Blocks Palette. That will show the variable's value on the Stage so you can see what's going on. You can also show the x and y coordinates and direction of a sprite by ticking the boxes beside them in the Motion blocks.

4 If you can't see all the blocks, you have selected the Stage next to the Sprite List. The Stage can't move and doesn't have a pen. Click one of your sprites in the Sprite List to bring back all the blocks.

5 To tidy up the Scripts Area, right-click on it and then choose cleanup from the menu. This lines up all your scripts and stops them overlapping.

6 Add comments to your script to help you to remember what it's doing, and what you need to do with it next. Right-click on the Scripts Area to add a comment box. Click the bottom-right corner to resize it, and drag it into the Blocks Palette to delete it.

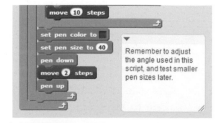

7 In Scratch 1.4, you can change the speed of the program so you can find bugs more easily. The option to do this is called single stepping. Click the **Edit** menu and choose **Set Single Stepping**. The options are Turbo (useful for testing programs that take a long time to run, but not often useful for games because you can't keep up on the controls); Normal (no different to running the script normally); Flash blocks (fast), which runs at normal speed but highlights each block as it runs; and Flash blocks (slow), which slows the program and highlights blocks as they run. You can turn single stepping on or off through the Edit menu. If you don't pick a speed first, it uses Flash blocks (slow).

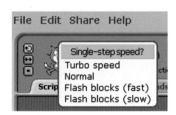

Hot tip

There's one block in Scratch 1.4 which I haven't covered in this book. It's the "forever if" Control block. It works the same as having an "if" block inside a "forever" block, so some people considered it pointless. Some people confused it with the "repeat until" block too. It was removed in Scratch 2.0, so even if you're using Scratch 1.4, I don't recommend you use this block.

8 In Scratch 2.0, there is a Turbo mode you can use to run your program (or any program) extremely fast. It can help you to identify problems with programs that take a long time to run. Hold down the Shift key and click the green flag to turn Turbo mode on or off. You can also enable it from the Edit menu.

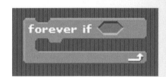

9 To track down a bug in a script, you can also try breaking it down into smaller pieces by stopping it early. You can use a Control block to stop the script or stop all scripts at any point in the program. When it finishes early, you can inspect the values of variables at that point by showing them on the Stage. Scratch 2.0 has a **stop** block with a menu in it to choose which scripts to stop. Scratch 1.4 has a block to stop the script the block is in, and one to stop all scripts.

207

Beware

As you try to fix your program, you might make it worse! Save a copy of it so you can always go back to the previous working version later (see Chapter 1).

Common bugs

Hot tip

Try reading your program aloud, or following its instructions with pen and paper. It can help you to spot problems with blocks being in the wrong order, or the wrong blocks being used together.

Every project is different, but there are a few bugs that come up more often than others:

- If your program isn't repeating things correctly, or isn't making decisions it should, check your Control blocks. When you have a complicated program, it's easy to end up with something inside the wrong bracket, but this completely changes the meaning of the program. Compare the two scripts below, and the shapes they create (shape pictures are not to the same scale):

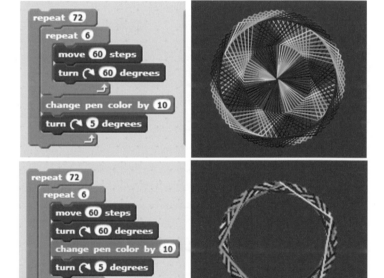

Beware

You can't divide a number by zero, so it will cause an error if you try.

- If a sprite sticks at the edge of the screen, check that you're not changing its coordinates to a position that is off the screen.

- Whenever you write a script, select the right sprite in the Sprite List first. If you need to copy a script from one sprite to another, click the script in the Scripts Area and drag it onto the other sprite in the Sprite List.

Hot tip

If you have problems with sprites not being synchronized with each other, use broadcasts (see Chapter 5).

- If you have an error that only occurs sometimes, check your variables and any blocks using random numbers.

Sharing your projects

There's a strong community around Scratch, built around sharing projects and feedback on them.

Sharing projects in Scratch 2.0 (web version)
To share a project in Scratch 2.0, click one of the **Share** buttons. You can find one in the top-right corner of the editor, and others in the My Stuff part of your profile.

When you click the button, your project is shared and you are taken to its project page. Add instructions, notes and credits, and up to three one-word tags, to help others to find your project.

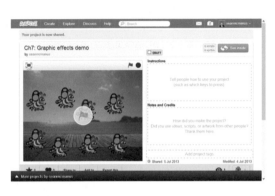

Sharing projects in Scratch 1.4
To share projects, you need to have an account for the Scratch website. If you don't already have one, see Chapter 2 for advice on creating one. To share a project in Scratch 1.4, click **Share** on the menu at the top of the screen and then click **Share This Project Online**. Enter your username and password, a name for the project, and some notes on it (including instructions if necessary). Tick the boxes on the left to choose up to three popular tags. Click the **OK** button and your project will be uploaded.

Receiving feedback
To see all the comments on your project, visit its project page on the Scratch website. You can find it by clicking your username in the top-right and then clicking **My Stuff**. Don't forget to leave feedback for others too. Click **Explore** at the top of the website to find projects and leave your comments under the project player.

Beware

When you share a Scratch project, you give everyone else permission to modify it and share their versions of it.

Beware

Because of copyright law, you're not allowed to use pictures or sounds you find online in the projects you share. The exception is if the person who made them has given you permission.

Resources/Acknowledgements

The Scratch website
http://scratch.mit.edu/

The author's website, including examples and bonus content
http://www.sean.co.uk

Search for free images and sounds you may use in your projects
http://search.creativecommons.org/

Scratch Wiki: a reference guide to Scratch
http://wiki.scratch.mit.edu/wiki/Scratch_Wiki

ScratchED: a community for educators using Scratch
http://scratched.media.mit.edu/

Raspberry Pi forums, including one dedicated to Scratch
http://www.raspberrypi.org/phpBB3/

Get a PicoBoard from Sparkfun Electronics (in the US)
https://www.sparkfun.com/products/10311

Get a PicoBoard from Proto-Pic (in the UK)
http://proto-pic.co.uk/picoboard/

Simon Walters' blog, including tutorials on ScratchGPIO
http://cymplecy.wordpress.com/scratch-raspberrypi-gpio/

To download the examples in this book, visit www.ineasysteps.com
Select Free Resources and then choose Downloads.

Acknowledgements
Scratch is developed by the Lifelong Kindergarten Group at the
MIT Media Lab. See **http://scratch.mit.edu**

Many thanks to those who helped with permissions and research
queries, including Mitchel Resnick, Liz Upton and Eben Upton
of The Raspberry Pi Foundation, Barnaby and Emily Kent of
Pi-Cars.com, Jan Boström, Tim Benson, Mike Cook and Simon
Walters. The webcam photo in Chapter 5 is courtesy of Logitech.

Special thanks to Karen McManus, who was a fantastic help
throughout this project, in particular with indexing and layout
into the In Easy Steps style.

About the author
Sean McManus is an expert technology author. His previous
books include Web Design in easy steps.

Hot tip

Visit the author's website
or **www.ineasysteps.
com/resources/
downloads** to find all
these links to save typing
them in!

210

Don't forget

If you enjoyed this book,
please blog about it
or write a review of it
on your favorite online
store! Thank you!

Index